Wonder-Under®

Sew No More Christmas Decor

Oxmoor House®

Wonder-Under® Sew No More Christmas Decor
from the *Fun with Fabric* series

©1998 by Oxmoor House, Inc.
Book Division of Southern Progress Corporation
P.O. Box 2463, Birmingham, Alabama 35201

Published by Oxmoor House, Inc., and Leisure Arts, Inc.

Library of Congress Catalog Number: 97-75836
Hardcover ISBN: 0-8487-1682-5
Softcover ISBN: 0-8487-1683-3
Manufactured in the United States of America
First Printing 1998

Editor-in-Chief: Nancy Fitzpatrick Wyatt
Senior Crafts Editor: Susan Ramey Cleveland
Senior Editor, Editorial Services: Olivia Kindig Wells
Art Director: James Boone

Wonder-Under® Sew No More Christmas Decor

Editor: Catherine Corbett Fowler
Editorial Assistant: Kaye Howard Smith
Copy Editor: L. Amanda Owens
Associate Art Director: Cynthia R. Cooper
Designer: Carol Damsky
Illustrator: Kelly Davis
Senior Photographer: John O'Hagan
Photographer: Keith Harrelson
Photo Stylist: Connie Formby
Senior Production Designer: Larry Hunter
Publishing Systems Administrator: Rick Tucker
Production Director: Phillip Lee
Associate Production Manager: Theresa L. Beste
Production Assistant: Faye Porter Bonner

We're Here For You!
We at Oxmoor House are dedicated to serving you with
reliable information that expands your imagination and
enriches your life. We welcome your comments and
suggestions. Please write us at:

Oxmoor House, Inc.
Editor, *Wonder-Under® Sew No More*
  Christmas Decor
2100 Lakeshore Drive
Birmingham, AL 35209

To order additional publications, call 1-205-877-6560.

Pellon and Wonder-Under are registered trademarks of
Freudenberg Nonwovens.

Contents

Page 30

Festive Furnishings

Wondrous Wearables

Traditional Trimmings

Glorious Gifts

Acknowledgments

Introduction

Roll out your ribbons, bring out your buttons, pick out your prints, and whip out your Wonder-Under®. **It's time for Christmas crafting the no-sew way!** Filled with fast-and-fabulous Christmas creations, *Wonder-Under® Sew No More Christmas Decor* shows you how to make holiday keepsakes for your home, tree, and friends as well as yourself.

The projects in this book have all been made with **Pellon® Wonder-Under®**, the leading brand of paper-backed fusible web. Therefore, *none* of the projects requires much time to create, and *none* of the projects requires sewing skills! You simply fuse your projects together! So if you find yourself longing to make special holiday decorations, gifts, and wearables but are hesitant to commit to time-consuming projects, we'll show you how to create beautiful holiday treasures quickly and easily.

We recognize that the holidays can be hectic and that you need to make the most of every moment, so we have filled the chapters in this book with treasures you can make in minutes yet enjoy for years.

★ Find ways to add yuletide flair to your home with simple fabric treatments in **Festive Furnishings.** From the kitchen to the den, discover projects that are the hallmark of holiday style.

★ Deck your walls, adorn your branches, encircle your tree, and enhance your hearth with the stunning decorations you associate with Christmas. They are all in **Traditional Trimmings.**

★ Shower friends and family with **Glorious Gifts** that are dressed up with a host of packaging ideas. You'll also find small, inexpensive gifts that are ideal for making in multiples.

★ Keep ease of construction foremost in mind with **Wondrous Wearables** that begin with plain purchased garments. All you have to do is embellish them with seasonal style.

So let's get started!
Turn the page—you're just in time to begin crafting for Christmas!

General Instructions

Pellon® Wonder-Under® is a paper-backed fusible web with a heat-activated adhesive and a temporary paper lining. A hot iron melts the glue, fusing fabrics together. The web holds fabrics in place and prevents raveling. With Wonder-Under, you don't have to sew a stitch!

Choosing the Correct Weight

Wonder-Under—Regular Weight and Heavy Duty—is available at fabric and crafts stores, off the bolt or in several prepackaged widths and lengths. It also comes in a ¾"-wide precut tape, 10 yards long, that is ideal for fusing hems and ribbons.

• Test different weights to find the Wonder-Under that best suits your project. Generally, you can use regular-weight web for medium- to lightweight fabrics. For heavyweight fabrics, a heavy-duty web is best. (Heavy Duty Wonder-Under has more glue and, therefore, more "stick.")

• For an appliquéd garment, heavy-duty web may add too much stiffness. Use regular-weight web and finish the edges of the appliqué as necessary to ensure a washable garment. (See the section on washable fabric paint under Embellishment Techniques on page 8.)

• For projects in this book, Regular Weight Wonder-Under is usually recommended, unless Heavy Duty is specified.

• The Wonder-Under package label gives tips on application and washability.

• Test Wonder-Under on scraps of fabric before you start your actual project. Let the sample cool and then check to see that the fabric pieces have bonded and that the fused layers won't separate.

Perfect Patterns

Wonder-Under is translucent, so you can place the web (paper side up) directly onto a pattern for tracing.

• If a pattern isn't the size you want, use a photocopier to enlarge or to reduce it.

• If a pattern has an asymmetrical or one-way design, the finished appliqué will be a mirror image of the pattern. So if a pattern points left, the appliqué will point right. **In this book, patterns are reversed as necessary.**

Fusing Basics

1. If the project you are making has an appliqué pattern, trace the pattern onto the paper (smooth) side of the Wonder-Under. Leaving a margin, cut around the shape.

2. For all Wonder-Under projects, place the web side of the Wonder-Under onto the wrong side of the fabric. Press for 5 seconds with a hot, dry iron. Let the fabric cool. (If some of the Wonder-Under sticks to your iron, remove it with a hot-iron cleaner, available in most notion departments of fabric and crafts stores.) For appliqués, cut out the shape along the pattern lines.

3. Remove the paper backing from the Wonder-Under.

4. Position the fabric, web side down, on your project. (Fusible items can be held temporarily in place by "touch basting." Touch the item to be fused with the tip of the iron only. If the item is not in the desired position, it can be lifted and repositioned.)

5. To fuse, cover the fabric with a damp pressing cloth, unless otherwise specified. Using an iron heated to the wool setting, press firmly for 10 seconds. (Heavy fabrics may require more time.) Repeat, lifting and overlapping the iron until all the fabric is fused.

6. Remove the pressing cloth and iron the fabric to eliminate excess moisture.

Embellishment Techniques

*D*etails, or embellishments, add a finishing touch to your project. They can also be functional. Pellon® Wonder-Under® holds appliqués securely in place, but some fraying may occur with frequent use. On such projects, consider adding a finish to fabric appliqués.

A good no-sew finish is **washable fabric paint.** Available at crafts stores, these paints come in squeeze tubes that allow you to apply a thin line of paint around an appliqué. Insert cardboard under the appliqué to catch seepage. Follow the manufacturer's directions for drying time; some paints require several days to set. Most manufacturers recommend washing the finished project in warm water.

If you prefer **a machine finish,** a decorative zigzag also adds security to edges. Closely spaced zigzag stitches—or satin stitching—give shapes strong definition and completely encase raw edges. Even multiple layers of fabric fused with Heavy Duty Wonder-Under can be effectively satin-stitched.

Buttons and beads create dimension and sparkle. Sewn or glued in place, they can represent ornaments, flower centers, and other details.

You can also glue **twine, rickrack, braid, lace, or other trims** to your project to give extra dimension and color.

Fine-tipped fabric markers are an easy way to add detail. You can use fine-tip markers to draw "quilting lines" around the edges of an appliqué. This technique is sometimes called pen stitching.

Festive Furnishings

On the following pages you will find projects to add Christmas cheer to every room in your house. From table coverings to rugs to lamps to pillows, we've got the theme for holiday home decor!

Page 14

Page 16

Page 21

Page 28

Handsome Holiday Table Covers

*D*rape your home with elegant fabric accents. Mix and match bold red-and-green prints with traditional Christmas plaids for an easy touch of holiday splendor.

Materials

For both:
¾"-wide Pellon® Wonder-Under® fusible tape
Fabric glue
For Table Skirt:
Fabric (See Step 1 for amount.)
For Table Topper:
Fabric (See Step 1 for amount.)
1¼ yards ¼"-diameter gold twisted cording
4 safety pins
4 (4¼"-long) gold tassels

Table Skirt Instructions

1. Referring to Diagram, measure table and drop length; add 40". Cut square of fabric equal to determined measurement. (If necessary, piece fabric by pressing fusible tape along 1 cut edge on right side. Remove paper backing. With right sides facing and edges aligned, fuse lengths of fabric together along edge. Press seam to 1 side.)

2. To hem table skirt, press fusible tape to wrong side of fabric square along each edge. Remove paper backing. Fold 1 edge of fabric to wrong side along inner edge of fusible tape. Fuse in place. Repeat for remaining edges. Secure corners with fabric glue.

3. Center skirt on table. Tuck edges of fabric under at floor and arrange folds for pouf effect.

Table Topper Instructions

1. Referring to Diagram, measure table and desired drop length of table topper; add 2". Cut square of fabric to determined measurement. (If necessary, use fusible tape to piece fabric as for Table Skirt.)

2. To hem table topper, repeat Step 2 for Table Skirt.

3. Cut cording into 4 (11¼") lengths. (To prevent ends of cording from fraying, before cutting apply fabric glue to ¼" of cording around area to be cut, let dry, and then cut.)

4. For each corner of topper, measure 9" from corner and gather fabric. Attach safety pin to wrong side of fabric to secure gathers. Wrap length of cording several times around gathered area. Secure with fabric glue.

5. Wrap hanging loop of tassel around wrapped cording and glue top of hanging loop to top of tassel. Let dry. Referring to photo, center table topper on top of table skirt.

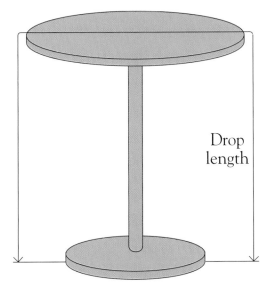

Drop length

Diagram

Fusible Facts

Some projects can be too large and unwieldy to work with on the ironing board. To create an extralarge work surface, lay a blanket or towels on a tabletop. Use an old sheet as a large pressing cloth.

Merry Mantel Scarf

*T*his holiday accent is made of individual panels, so you can customize the scarf to fit your mantel. Simple braided trim and gold tassels provide an elegant finishing touch.

Materials

Fabric (See steps 1 and 2 for amount.)
¾"-wide Pellon® Wonder-Under® fusible tape
Fabric marking pencil
Hot-glue gun and glue sticks
¼"-wide gold trim
6½"-long gold tassels (1 for each panel)
¾" x ⅞" oval jewel shank buttons (1 for each panel)
Drapery weights (2 for each panel)

Instructions

Note: If using fabric with repeated pattern, carefully match fabric pattern across panels.

1. **To determine number of panels needed for scarf,** measure front edge of mantel for desired finished length of scarf. From this measurement, determine desired finished width of each panel. (For best results, choose panel width that will divide evenly into finished scarf length. Our 62½"-long scarf is made up of 5 [12½"-wide] panels.) Divide finished scarf length by finished panel width.

2. **For each panel,** to determine width of fabric piece for panel, add 4" to finished panel width. To determine length of fabric piece for panel, measure from back of mantel to desired finished drop length of panel (point of panel without tassel); add 2". Cut piece of fabric to determined measurements.

3. For 1" double hem along each long side edge of fabric piece, press side edges of fabric 1" to wrong side. Press fusible tape along pressed edges. Remove paper backing. Fold each side edge 1" to wrong side again and fuse in place. Repeat to hem 1 short edge (top edge) of fabric piece.

4. For point, referring to Diagram A, press bottom corners of fabric piece diagonally to wrong side. Use fabric marking pencil to mark dot at point and at top of each side edge of point. Unfold fabric.

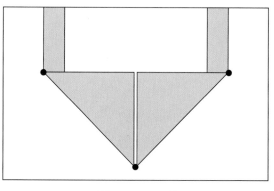

Diagram A

5. Referring to Diagram B, press fusible tape along bottom raw edge of fabric piece and along each side edge from marked dot to first length of fusible tape. Remove paper backing. Fold bottom corners diagonally to wrong side as before. Fuse in place.

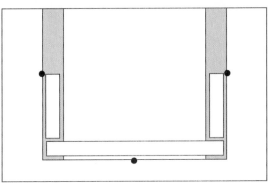

Diagram B

6. Hot-glue trim along edges on right side of panel. Hot-glue hanging loop of tassel to wrong side of panel at point and glue button to point above tassel. Hot-glue a drapery weight to each top corner on wrong side of panel. Let dry.

7. Arrange panels with top edge of each panel along back edge of mantel.

Santa Cane Place Mat

A clever appliqué adds a jolly accent to a purchased place mat. If you can't find a mat you like, make your own by simply hemming the edges of a 15" x 20½" piece of fabric with paper-backed fusible tape.

Materials

Purchased place mat (at least 11½" wide along short edges)

Fabrics for appliqués: 5" x 12" piece red-and-white striped; 4" x 6" piece white; 2" square each flesh-colored, pink, and gold; ½" x 2½" torn strip white

7" x 11" piece Pellon® Heavy Duty Wonder-Under®

Hot-glue gun and glue sticks

⅜"-diameter red shank button for nose

Permanent black fabric markers: fine-point, medium-point

Instructions

1. Wash and dry place mat and fabrics several times to preshrink as much as possible. Press.

2. Trace 1 candy cane, 2 cheeks (1 in reverse), 1 star, 1 hat trim, 1 beard, and 1 face on page 18 onto paper side of Wonder-Under. Leaving approximate ½" margin, cut around each shape.

3. Press candy cane shape onto wrong side of red-and-white striped fabric, hat trim and beard onto wrong side of 4" x 6" piece of white fabric, face onto wrong side of flesh-colored fabric, cheeks onto wrong side of pink fabric, and star onto wrong side of gold fabric. Cut out shapes along pattern lines. Remove paper backing.

4. Referring to photo, arrange appliqué shapes on right-hand side of place mat, overlapping shapes as necessary. Fuse in place.

5. For mustache, pinch torn white fabric strip at center to gather. Hot-glue center of strip just above beard. Hot-glue button to center of mustache. Trim ends of mustache as desired.

6. Using fine-point permanent marker, draw stitching lines along edges of candy cane and hat trim. Using medium-point permanent marker, draw dots for eyes and stitching lines along edges of star.

Other Ideas

To create a place-setting ensemble, fuse a Santa cane appliqué to a set of plain cloth napkins. Or if you prefer, fuse the motif to the front of a bright cloth dish towel.

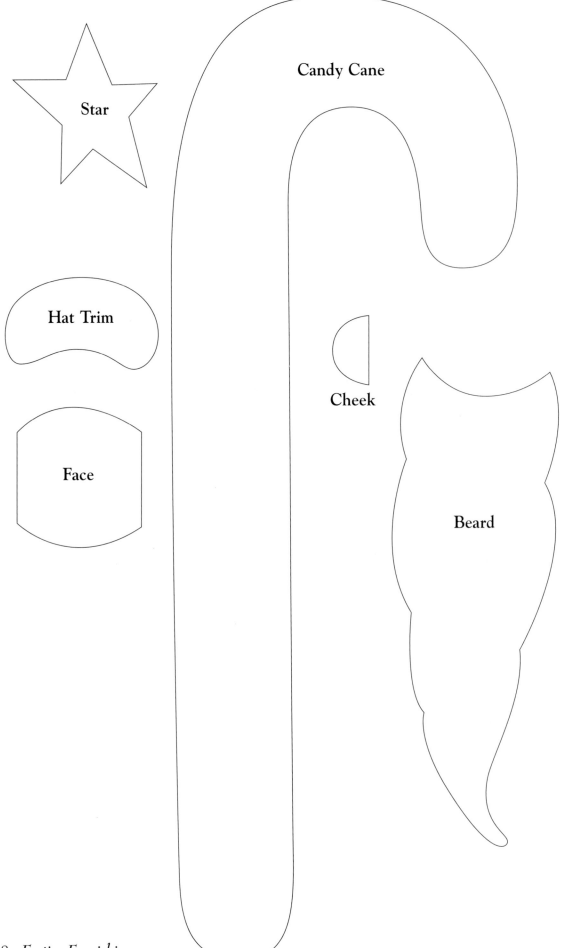

Star

Candy Cane

Hat Trim

Cheek

Face

Beard

Woodland Log Tote

This attractive and functional firewood carrier is a snap to make. Either start with a purchased tote or follow our easy instructions to make your own.

Materials

- ¼ yard Pellon® Heavy Duty Wonder-Under®
- Green, red, and blue checked flannel scraps
- Purchased log tote*
- Gold dimensional fabric paint in squeeze bottle (optional)
- Gold thread (optional)
- Size 100 sewing machine needle (optional)

* To make your own tote, you will need 1 yard of canvas, 2¾ yards of 1"-wide belt webbing, and thread to match canvas and webbing.

Instructions

Note: To make your own tote, follow steps 3–5.

1. Trace 3 trees onto paper side of Wonder-Under. Leaving approximate ½" margin, cut around shapes. Press 1 tree shape onto wrong side of each flannel scrap. Cut out shapes along pattern lines. Remove paper backing.

2. If using purchased tote, referring to photo, arrange tree shapes along 1 end of log tote, overlapping as necessary. Fuse in place.

3. If making your own tote, cut 2 (16" x 34") rectangles from canvas. Referring to photo, arrange trees at center top of 1 canvas piece, leaving 4" margin on both sides and 1¾" margin at top. Fuse in place.

4. To sew tote, using ½" seam allowance and thread to match canvas, with right sides facing and raw edges aligned, machine-stitch canvas rectangles together, leaving 4" opening for turning. Trim corners and grade seam allowances. Turn and press. Topstitch ¼" and then ½" along all sides.

5. To make handles, beginning on back side of tote and using thread to match belt webbing, stitch webbing to canvas 2¼" from outside edges, leaving approximately 16" of webbing at each end for handles. Where webbing ends meet, turn top piece under ¼" and overlap ends. Stitch in place. Reinforce handles by stitching over previous topstitching.

6. For either purchased or made tote, outline appliqués with dimensional paint. Let dry. Alternately, for added security, use gold thread to machine-satin-stitch along edges of appliqués, using size 100 sewing machine needle and widest zigzag stitch. Reduce stitch width at angled points and indentations.

Tree

Patchwork Pillows

$\mathcal{I}$t's easy to bring a bit of homespun warmth to your Christmas decor with these patchwork pillows. No one will believe that you made them without sewing a stitch!

Materials

For each:
Pellon® Wonder-Under®
¾" Pellon® Wonder-Under® fusible tape

For Bear's Paw Pillow:
Fabrics: coordinating scraps for appliqués, 13½" square for background, 2 (20") squares for pillow front and back
18" square pillow form

For Forest Pillow:
Fabrics: scraps for appliqués, 14½" square for background, 29" square for pillow back, coordinating pieces for border (See Border Chart on page 23 for amounts.)
29" square muslin
26" square pillow form

Bear's Paw Pillow Instructions

1. Cut 1 (8½") square each from 1 appliqué fabric and Wonder-Under. Press Wonder-Under square onto wrong side of fabric square. Remove paper backing. Center and press 8½" square onto right side of 13½" background square.

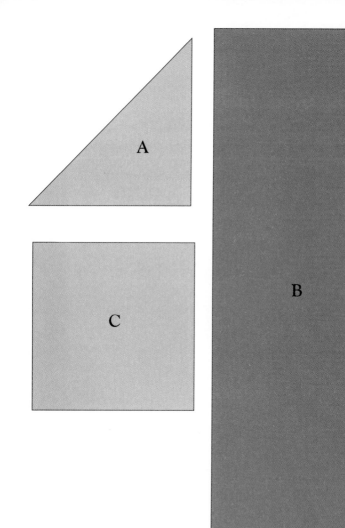

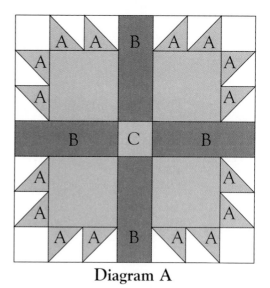

Diagram A

2. Spacing shapes at least 1" apart, trace 16 As, 4 Bs, and 1 C onto paper side of Wonder-Under. Leaving approximate ½" margin, cut around each shape.

3. Press shapes onto wrong side of appliqué fabrics. Cut out shapes along pattern lines. Do *not* remove paper backing. Press 1 short end of each shape B ½" to wrong side.

4. Cut 1 (13½") square from Wonder-Under. Press Wonder-Under square onto wrong side of 13½" background square. Do not remove paper backing. Press each edge of background square ¾" to wrong side.

5. Remove paper backing from shapes A, B, and C. Referring to Diagram A, arrange shapes on background square with pressed end of each shape B folded over pressed edge of background square. Press in place.

6. Remove paper backing from background square. Press fusible tape along pressed edges of background square, being careful not to let iron touch exposed Wonder-Under. Remove paper backing. Center and fuse background square onto right side of 1 (20") square of fabric.

7. Press fusible tape along edges of both 20" squares on right side of fabric. Remove paper backing from bottom and side edges *only*. With right sides facing, fuse bottom and side edges of squares together; clip corners. Carefully turn right side out. Insert pillow form.

8. Remove paper backing from fusible tape along top edges. Fold edges to inside and pin together. Fuse in place, removing pins as you fuse.

Forest Pillow Instructions

1. Spacing shapes at least 1" apart, trace each star twice and each tree once onto paper side of Wonder-Under. Leaving approximate ½" margin, cut around shapes.

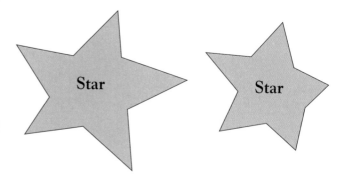

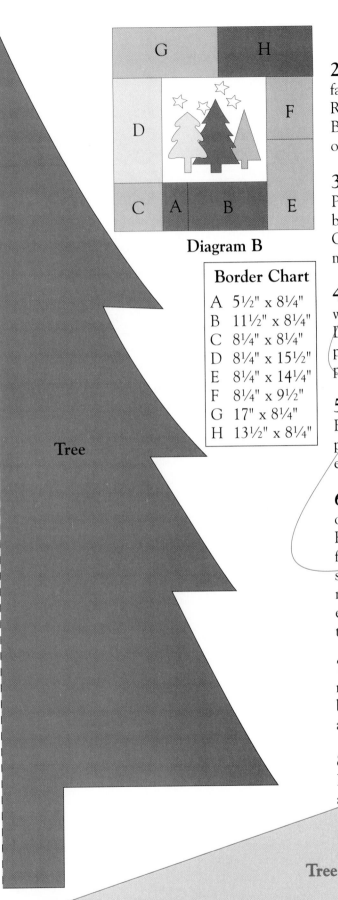

Tree

Tree

Diagram B

Border Chart		
A	5½" x 8¼"	
B	11½" x 8¼"	
C	8¼" x 8¼"	
D	8¼" x 15½"	
E	8¼" x 14¼"	
F	8¼" x 9½"	
G	17" x 8¼"	
H	13½" x 8¼"	

Tree

2. Press shapes onto wrong side of appliqué fabrics. Cut out shapes along pattern lines. Remove paper backing. Referring to Diagram B, arrange shapes on 14½" background square, overlapping as necessary. Fuse in place.

3. Cut 1 (14½") square from Wonder-Under. Press Wonder-Under square onto wrong side of background square. Remove paper backing. Center and fuse background square onto muslin square.

4. For border, press Wonder-Under onto wrong side of border fabrics. Referring to Diagram B and Border Chart, cut designated pieces from border fabrics. Do not remove paper backing.

5. Press fusible tape onto right side of pieces B, C, E, and H along 1 (8¼") side. For each piece, press edge to wrong side along inner edge of fusible tape. Remove paper backing.

6. Referring to Diagram B, place pressed edge of B over A, overlapping ¾". Fuse in place. Repeat to fuse C to D, E to F, and H to G, forming 4 strips. Press fusible tape onto right side of each strip along 1 long edge. Do *not* remove paper backing. For each strip, press edge to wrong side along inner edge of fusible tape. Remove paper backing.

7. Referring to Diagram B, arrange strips on muslin, placing pressed edges over edges of background square and raw edges under an adjoining strip. Fuse in place.

8. To complete pillow, follow steps 7 and 8 of Bear's Paw Pillow, using 29" square of fabric and pillow top.

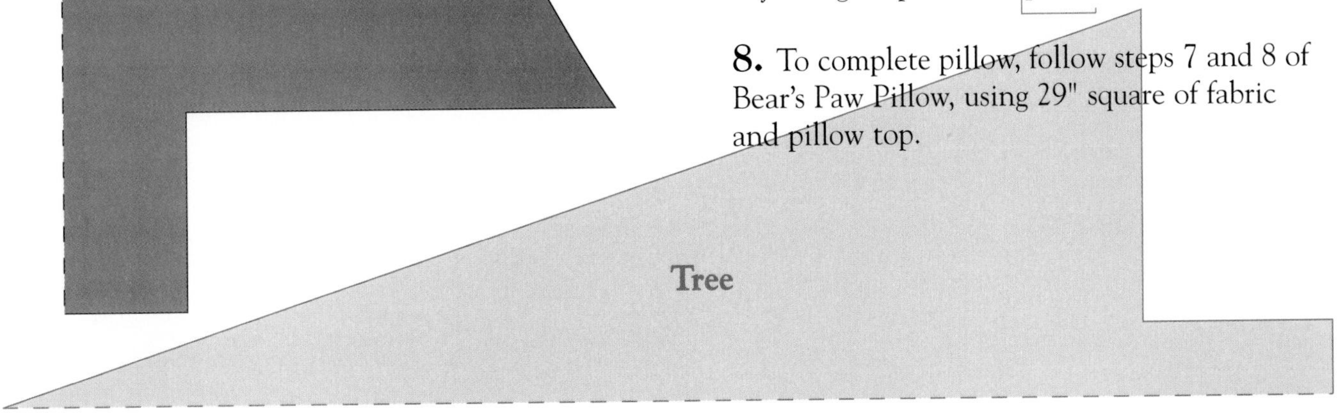

Tapestry Rug

$\mathcal{R}$ich red and green tapestries are readily available as the holiday season approaches. Showcase one of these beautiful fabrics by transforming a length into a stunning throw rug.

Materials
Tapestry fabric in desired size (We used a 40" x 54" piece.)
¾"-wide Pellon® Wonder-Under® fusible tape
6" bullion fringe (See Step 3 for amount.)
Aluminum foil
Hot-glue gun and glue sticks
Clothespins (optional)

Instructions

1. Press fabric. Even up edges of fabric, centering design if necessary.

2. Press fusible tape onto wrong side of fabric along each long edge. Remove paper backing. Fold 1 long edge of fabric to wrong side along inner edge of fusible tape. Fuse in place. Repeat for remaining long edge.

3. For fringe, measure 1 short end of fabric; add 3". Cut 2 lengths of fringe to determined measurement.

4. Cover work surface with aluminum foil to protect it. Beginning 1½" from cut end of fringe, glue 1 length of fringe to right side of 1 short end of fabric. Fold cut ends of fringe to wrong side and hot-glue in place. If necessary, hold fringe in place with clothespins until glue dries. Repeat to attach remaining length of fringe to remaining short end.

Fusible Fact

Fusible adhesive works with both the heat and the pressure of an iron. If you are having trouble getting your fabric to adhere, try these tips to get a better bond.
- Raise the temperature of the iron and fuse again.
- Hold the iron in place longer.
- Apply more pressure to the iron.
- Check if the fabric has a protective finish. Fusible adhesives can't penetrate protective coatings such as Scotchguard®. Rayon and acetate are also resistant to fusible adhesives.

Cardinal Place Mat

The brilliant red plumage of the cardinal adds a splash of color to winter white.
Adorn your table with a whole flock of mats.

Materials

⅜"-wide green grosgrain ribbon
Fabric glue
Purchased fabric place mat
Lightweight fusible interfacing
Fabrics: 7" square red print, scraps of
    green, 7" square white for bird
    appliqué backing
Pellon® Wonder-Under®
Black dimensional fabric paint in
    squeeze bottle

Instructions

1. Glue ribbon to place mat ⅛" from edges, mitering ribbon at corners. Let dry.

2. Fuse interfacing onto wrong side of fabrics. Trace bird, leaves, and berries patterns onto paper side of Wonder-Under. Leaving approximate ½" margin, cut around shapes. Remove paper backing. Referring to photo for colors, press shapes onto wrong side of fabrics. Cut out shapes along pattern lines.

3. Fuse bird onto center of white fabric. Using fabric paint, paint over raw edges of bird; paint beak and details. Let dry. Cut out bird close to painted lines.

4. Position bird on place mat with tail extending approximately ½" beyond edge. Referring to photo, position leaves and berries below bird. Fuse in place. Glue bird in place. Using fabric paint, paint over raw edges of leaves and berries. Let dry.

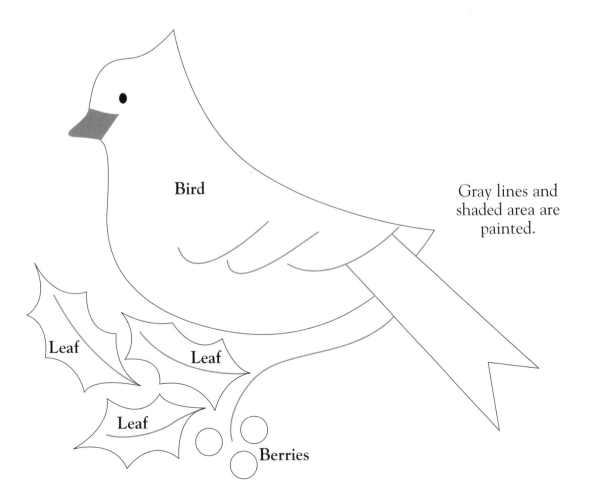

Bird

Gray lines and
shaded area are
painted.

Leaf

Leaf

Leaf

Berries

Heavenly Light

*L*et your Christmas spirit shine! Fuse angel appliqués to a fabric-covered lampshade and then attach it to your favorite lamp.

Materials

- Purchased fabric-covered lampshade
- Fabric: strips to wrap around top and bottom of lampshade (See Step 1 for amounts.), scraps for appliqués
- Pellon® Wonder-Under®
- Fabric glue
- Fine-tip permanent black fabric marker

Instructions

1. Measure around top and bottom edges of lampshade. Cut 1 (4"-wide) strip of fabric to each measurement. Press Wonder-Under onto wrong side of each fabric strip. Remove paper backing.

2. For each strip, fold 1" of each long edge to Wonder-Under side of strip. (Cut edges should meet at center of strip.) Fuse in place. Encase top edge of lampshade in corresponding fabric strip. Glue fabric strip in place. Repeat for bottom edge of lampshade with remaining strip.

3. Trace star A, star B, head, wings, hands, angel body, and feet patterns onto paper side of Wonder-Under as many times as desired. Leaving approximate ½" margin, cut around shapes. Remove paper backing. Referring to photo for colors, press Wonder-Under shapes onto wrong side of fabric scraps. Cut out shapes along pattern lines.

4. Referring to photo, fuse angel shapes onto lampshade in order indicated. Fuse star shapes onto lampshade between angels.

5. Using permanent marker, outlines shapes and draw details.

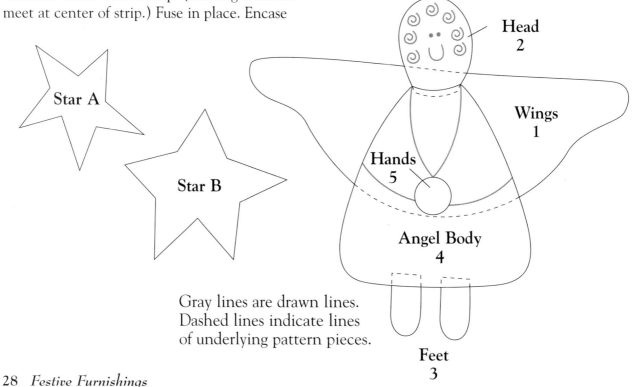

Gray lines are drawn lines.
Dashed lines indicate lines of underlying pattern pieces.

North Woods Throw

Dressed up with fused fabric appliqués, this rustic throw is a handsome accent for a hearthside chair. Begin with a purchased polar fleece blanket, and you will be snuggling under its folds in no time!

Materials

- ½ yard Pellon® Heavy Duty Wonder-Under®
- Felt: 8" x 10" piece tan; 1 (6") square each yellow, black, and green
- Purchased polar fleece throw with blanket-stitched edging
- Black dimensional fabric paint in squeeze bottle
- Embroidery needle (optional)
- Black pearl cotton (optional)

Instructions

Note: To prevent crushing pile of throw when fusing appliqués, cover appliqués with press cloth and hold iron just above shapes. Do not set weight of iron on appliqués. Use lots of steam to fuse shapes in place.

1. Trace 1 moose and 1 reversed moose onto paper side of Wonder-Under; also draw 1 (3") square, 1 (4") square, and 1 (5") square. Center and draw tree shape on diagonal of 5" square; draw diagonal line across remaining 2 squares. Leaving approximate ½" margin, cut around moose and squares.

2. Press each moose onto tan felt, 3" square onto yellow felt, 4" square onto black felt, and 5" square onto green felt. Cut out shapes along pattern lines. Cut tree shape from center of 5" square, making sure not to cut from an outside edge. Cut remaining squares in half along diagonal lines. Remove paper backing.

3. Referring to photo, center and fuse shapes in place along 1 end of throw, positioning so that bottom edges are approximately 5" from bottom edge of throw.

4. Use fabric paint to outline shapes and to draw blanket stitches along edges. Let dry. If you prefer, for added security, use pearl cotton to stitch blanket stitches along edges of appliqués.

Moose
Transfer.
Reverse and
transfer again.

Tree

Place on fold.

Homespun Towels

Since you spend much of the holidays in the kitchen, don't forget to whip up some yuletide cheer for that room. These towels make a quick decorating accent. Because kitchen towels often come several to a package, they are also economical Christmas gifts to make in multiples.

Materials (for 1 towel)

Kitchen towel
Fabrics for appliqués
Pellon® Heavy Duty Wonder-Under®
Dimensional fabric paints in squeeze
   bottle: bronze, gold, black

Instructions

1. Wash and dry towel and fabrics. Do not use fabric softener in washer or dryer. Press.

2. Trace desired patterns onto paper side of Wonder-Under. Leaving approximate ½" margin, cut around shapes. Press shapes onto wrong side of appliqué fabrics. Cut out shapes along pattern lines. Remove paper backing.

3. Referring to photo, arrange shapes on towel, overlapping as necessary. Fuse in place.

4. Referring to photo and using bronze dimensional paint, outline angel dress, angel wings, partridge, and pear; add details to pear. Let dry. Using gold dimensional paint, outline angel heart and leaves; draw leaf veins. Let dry. Using black dimensional paint, outline angel hair, angel face, angel legs, partridge wing, and branch; draw angel eyes, partridge eye, partridge beak, partridge plume, and pear stem. Let dry.

Angel Hair

Angel Face

Angel Dress

Angel Wing
Transfer. Reverse
and transfer again.

Angel Legs

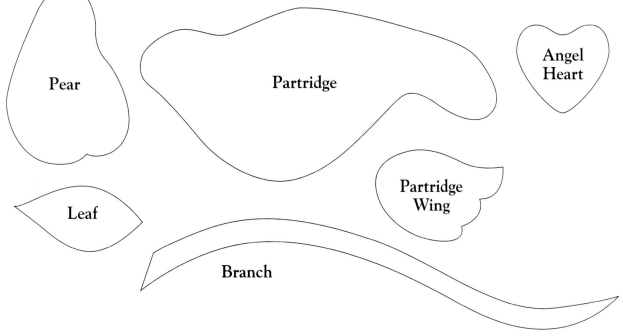

Pear

Partridge

Angel
Heart

Leaf

Partridge
Wing

Branch

Regal Table Runner

A festive decoration when serving a holiday buffet, this runner adorns only the center length of your serving area, so you still have ample room for chafing dishes and platters.

Materials

Fabric (See Step 1 for amount.)
Fabric marking pencil
¾"-wide Pellon® Wonder-Under® fusible tape
Fabric glue
⅝"-wide gold scalloped trim
1½ yards 1½"-wide gold mesh wire-edged ribbon
2 safety pins

Instructions

1. Determine desired finished length of table runner and add 1½". Cut fabric 16½" wide by augmented length.

2. Referring to Diagram, use fabric marking pencil to draw point on wrong side of fabric at each end. Cut fabric along drawn lines.

3. To hem table runner, press fusible tape to wrong side of fabric along each edge. Remove paper backing. Fold 1 edge of fabric to wrong side along inner edge of fusible tape. Fuse in place. Repeat for remaining edges. Secure corners with fabric glue.

4. Beginning and ending at 1 end of runner, glue trim along edges on wrong side, positioning so that scalloped edge of trim extends beyond edges of runner.

5. For bows, cut ribbon length in half. Tie each length in bow. Trim ends as shown in photo. Using safety pin on wrong side of runner, pin a bow to each end of runner.

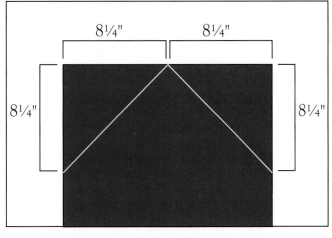

Diagram

Traditional Trimmings

Christmas just wouldn't be
Christmas without ornaments
and tree skirts, stockings and
wreaths. Look no further than
this chapter to find all of
these items—and more!

Page 52

Page 55

Page 66

Page 69

Ho, Ho, Ho Wall Hanging

Special touches make this banner thoroughly charming. The two-tone star gives depth, and the pom-pom on the tip of Santa's hat, the button ornaments, and the rickrack trim add dimension.

Materials

Lightweight fusible interfacing
Fabrics: 18¼" x 22½" piece red-and-white stripe for background; 22¼" x 26½" piece red print for outer border; 14" x 23" piece gold for inner border; scraps of light gold, dark gold, red, white, peach, green, and plaid for appliqués; 3½" x 17" strip muslin for hanging sleeve
Pellon® Wonder-Under®
¾"-wide Pellon® Wonder-Under® fusible tape
2½ yards white rickrack
Hot-glue gun and glue sticks
11 various red and white buttons
1"-diameter white pom-pom
Medium-tip permanent black fabric marker
17" length ¼"-diameter wooden dowel

Instructions

1. From interfacing, cut 1 (18¼" x 22½") piece and 1 (22¼" x 26½") piece. Fuse corresponding interfacing pieces to wrong side of background fabric and outer border fabric.

2. From Wonder-Under, cut 1 (18¼" x 22½") piece and 1 (14" x 23") piece. Press corresponding Wonder-Under pieces onto wrong side of background fabric piece and inner border fabric piece. Do not remove paper backing.

3. From inner border fabric piece, cut 2 (3½" x 18¼") strips and 2 (3½" x 22½") strips. Remove paper backing. With edges aligned, fuse long inner border strips to long edges of background fabric piece; fuse short inner border strips to short edges of background fabric.

4. Cut 2" square from each corner of outer border fabric piece. Remove paper backing from background fabric piece. Center and fuse background fabric piece to wrong side of outer border fabric piece.

5. Press fusible tape along 1 long edge on wrong side of outer border fabric piece. Remove paper backing. Referring to Diagram, fold and fuse 2" of outer border to wrong side, covering edge of inner border. Repeat for remaining long edge and then short edges of outer border fabric piece.

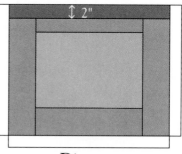

Diagram

6. Trace 3 of each letter on page 41 onto paper side of Wonder-Under. Trace 1 of

remaining shapes, except star, onto paper side of Wonder-Under. For star, trace 1 entire shape and then 1 of each shaded area onto paper side of Wonder-Under. Leaving approximate ½" margin, cut around shapes.

7. For star, press entire Wonder-Under star shape onto wrong side of light gold fabric scrap. Press Wonder-Under shaded area shapes onto wrong side of dark gold fabric scrap. Cut out shapes along pattern lines. Remove paper backing from shaded area shapes *only*. Referring to pattern, press shaded area shapes onto right side of entire star shape. Remove paper backing from star shape.

8. Referring to photo for colors, press remaining Wonder-Under shapes onto wrong side of corresponding fabric scraps. Cut out shapes along pattern lines. Remove paper backing. Overlapping appliqués as needed, arrange shapes on wall hanging (see photo). Fuse in place.

9. For hanging sleeve, press short edges and then long edges of muslin strip ½" to wrong side. Press fusible tape along each long pressed edge on wrong side. Remove paper backing. With wrong sides together, center sleeve on back of wall hanging, approximately ½" from top edge. Fuse in place.

10. Hot-glue rickrack along inner edges of outer border, trimming to fit (see photo). Hot-glue buttons to tree and pom-pom to point of hat. Using black marker, draw eyes on face. To hang, insert dowel into hanging sleeve.

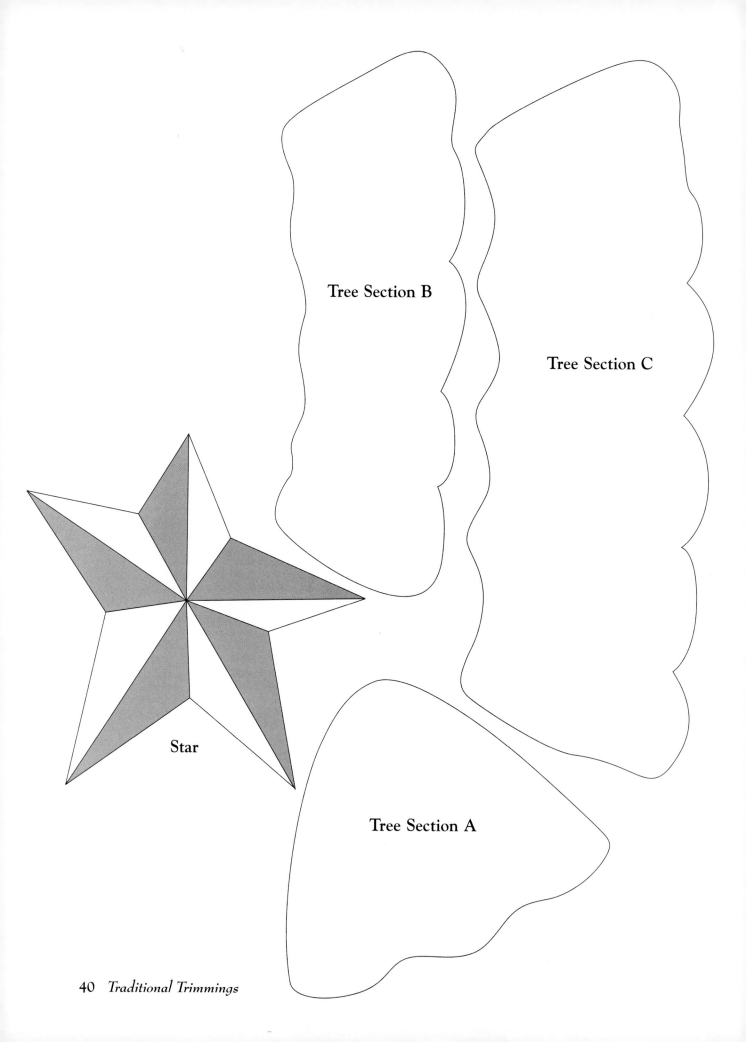

Tree Section B

Tree Section C

Star

Tree Section A

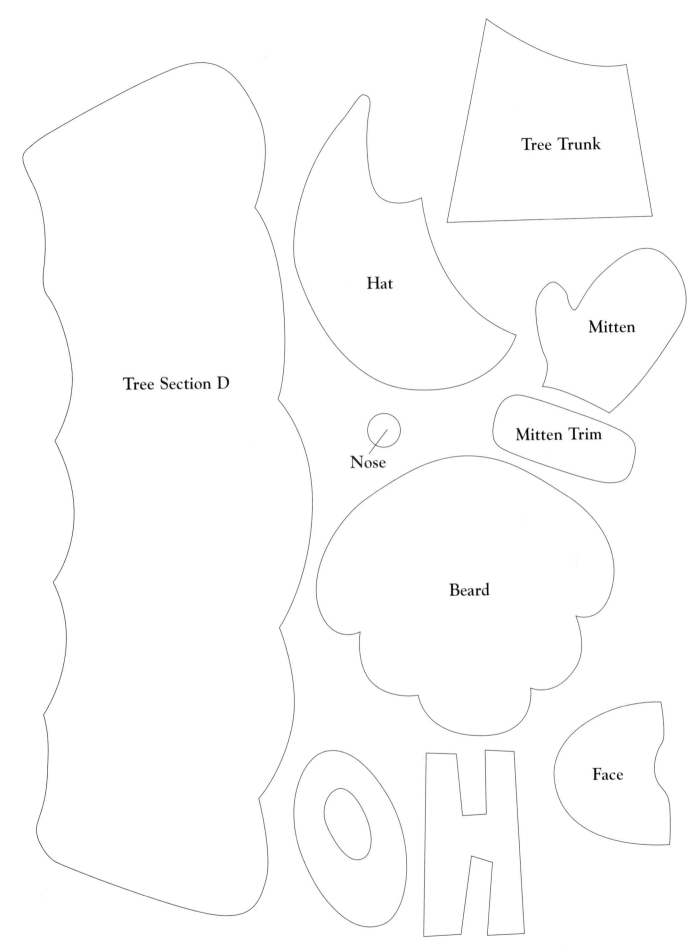

Tree Trunk

Hat

Mitten

Tree Section D

Mitten Trim

Nose

Beard

Face

Buttons & Birds Tree Skirt

This tree skirt could not be quicker or easier to create. A simple stencil makes the design a cinch to paint, and pinked felt creates a no-fuss finished edge.

Materials

Pellon® Wonder-Under®
40" square fabric
String
Fabric marking pencil
Thumbtack
Pinking shears
42" square felt to coordinate with
    fabric
Acetate for stencil
Fine-tip permanent black fabric marker
Cutting mat or thick layer of
    newspaper
Craft knife
Transparent tape (optional)
Acrylic paints: red, green
2 stencil brushes
Paper towels
5 (⅝") buttons
Hot-glue gun and glue sticks

Instructions

1. Press Wonder-Under onto wrong side of fabric square, piecing as necessary. Remove paper backing. With right sides facing, fold fabric square in half from top to bottom and then again from left to right.

2. To mark outer cutting line, tie 1 end of string to fabric marking pencil. Measure and mark string 18" from pencil; insert thumbtack into string at this point. Referring to Diagram, insert thumbtack into fabric and mark quarter-circle. To mark inner cutting line, repeat, inserting thumbtack into string 1½" from pencil.

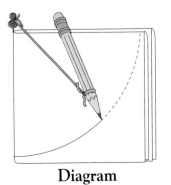

Diagram

3. Cutting through all layers of fabric, use pinking shears to cut out fabric along marked lines.

4. Fuse fabric skirt to felt square. Using pinking shears, trim felt even with center opening in skirt and ½" from outer edge of skirt. For opening in back, fold skirt in half. Cut along 1 fold from outer edge to center opening.

5. For stencil, cut piece of acetate 1" larger on all sides than entire pattern on page 44. Center acetate on top of pattern and use permanent marker to trace pattern. Place acetate piece on cutting mat and use craft knife to cut out stencil, making sure edges are smooth.

6. Position stencil straight up and down, with bottom of heart ½" from outer edge of fabric. Hold or tape stencil in place. Referring to photo for colors and using clean, dry stencil brush for each color, dip brush into paint and remove excess on paper towel. Brush should be almost dry for best results. Beginning at edge of cutout area, apply paint in stamping motion. Carefully remove stencil and let paint dry. Clean stencil and turn stencil over. With stencil heart positioned over painted heart, stencil remaining half of design.

7. Leaving approximately 2¼" between designs, repeat Step 6 to stencil design 5 more times along outer edge of skirt.

8. Using permanent fabric marker, outline designs and draw stitching lines close to edges of hearts, birds, and leaves.

9. Hot-glue 1 button to center of each whole heart.

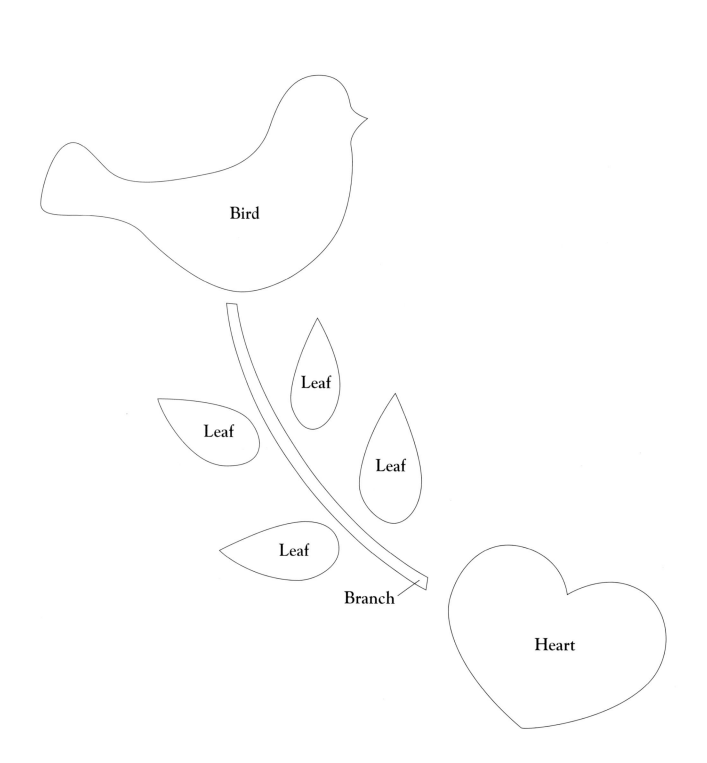

Bird

Leaf

Leaf

Leaf

Leaf

Branch

Heart

Quilts on the Line

Add homespun charm to your Christmas tree with these patchwork blocks. Color the blocks with permanent markers and embellish them with your favorite fabric scraps. Clip the mini quilts to a clothesline garland or hang them from your tree.

Materials (for 3 blocks)

Tracing paper or other thin paper
Manila folder
Carbon paper
Fine-tip permanent markers in colors
    to coordinate with fabrics
Ruler
Pellon® Wonder-Under® scraps
Fabric scraps for corner blocks
    and borders
Cotton cording for clothesline
Miniature spring-type clothespins

Instructions

1. For each, trace desired quilt block design onto tracing paper. Layer manila folder, carbon paper (carbon side down), and tracing-paper design. Retrace quilt block design to transfer to manila folder. Referring to photo for inspiration and using permanent markers, color quilt block.

2. Using pencil and ruler, draw box 1" outside quilt block design. Cut out design along drawn lines.

3. Press Wonder-Under onto wrong side of corner block and border fabrics. Cut 4 (1") squares from corner block fabric and 4 (1" x 5") strips from border fabric. Remove paper backing.

4. Referring to photo, fuse border fabric strips along edges of each manila square, overlapping ends at corners. Fuse corner blocks to corners.

5. For clothesline, cut desired length of cording and knot ends. Use clothespins to hang ornaments from cording.

Other Ideas

Create Christmas greetings that will thrill any quilter. Enlarge these traditional quilting patterns, cut the pieces from Christmas fabrics, and then fuse them to the front of plain note cards.

Virginia Star

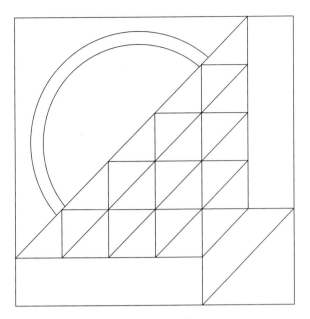

Cherry Basket

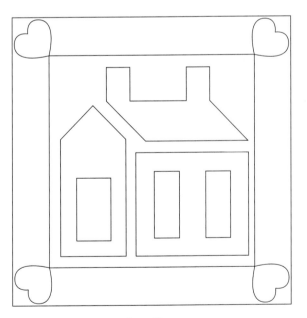

Schoolhouse

Measuring Tree

$\mathcal{R}$ecord your kids' growth between Christmases. Paint their names and corresponding heights along with the year on felt ornaments and then hang the ornaments at the appropriate measurements. You may be surprised at how quickly your little ones reach the top boughs of the tree!

Materials

Pellon® Heavy Duty Wonder-Under®
Felt: ½ yard each 45"-wide green and red, 12" square blue, 5" x 10½" piece black, 3½" x 10½" piece yellow
Pinking shears
¾"-wide Pellon® Wonder-Under® fusible tape
1½ yards yellow jumbo rickrack
Thick craft glue
Dimensional fabric paints in squeeze bottle
17" length ¼"-diameter wooden dowel
28" length white yarn

Instructions

1. Trace triangle pattern (page 51) 5 times and star pattern (page 50) 1 time onto paper side of Wonder-Under. Then draw 1 (5" x 6") rectangle on paper side of Wonder-Under. Leaving approximate ½" margin, cut around shapes. Press triangle shapes onto green felt and star shape onto blue felt. Press rectangle shape onto black felt. Cut out shapes along pattern lines. Remove paper backing.

2. Using pinking shears, cut 1 (13½" x 45") piece from red felt. Using regular scissors, cut 3 (3"-diameter) circles each from red, blue, and yellow felt; cut 9 (1" x 1¾") rectangles from black felt.

3. For growth chart casing, cut 13½" length of fusible tape. Press fusible tape along 1 short end of red felt. Remove paper backing. Fold end down 3" and fuse in place.

4. For tree trunk, center 5" x 6" black felt rectangle on front of growth chart, positioning so that 1 (6") edge is 1½" from bottom edge of chart. Fuse in place.

5. Center and fuse 1 green triangle on black rectangle, overlapping top of rectangle 1½". Center and fuse another triangle on top of first triangle, overlapping tip of first triangle 2". In same manner, continue centering and fusing remaining triangles. Center and fuse star on top of tree.

6. Referring to photo, cut lengths of yellow rickrack and glue 1 to each triangle. Let dry.

7. To make ornaments, referring to photo, glue 1 (1" x 1¾") black rectangle to each circle, positioning so that half of rectangle extends off edge of circle.

8. Measure and mark 6" from bottom edge of growth chart. Using dimensional fabric paint in desired color, paint dot ¾" from right edge of chart at mark. Measure 6" from this point and mark with dot. Paint "3" next to this dot. Continue in same manner, measuring and marking at 6" intervals, to designate 4' and 5' levels. Let dry.

9. Run dowel through casing. Center growth chart on dowel. Tie ends of yarn length to dowel next to growth chart (see photo).

10. Hang growth chart on wall 2' above floor. Use dimensional fabric paint to paint child's name and height along with the year on each ornament. Let dry. Glue ornament to tree at appropriate measurement.

Star

To accurately measure your child's height, hang the tree 2' above the floor.

Triangle

Place on fold.

Yuletide Card Holder

Store all the greeting cards you receive throughout the holidays in this clever holder. Each pocket will hold cards up to 5" wide.

Materials

Pellon® Heavy Duty Wonder-Under®
17½" x 45" piece heavy muslin
¾"-wide Pellon® Heavy Duty Wonder-Under® fusible tape
Ruler
Fine-tip permanent black fabric marker
Fabrics for appliqués
Graphite transfer paper
Hot-glue gun and glue sticks
6 assorted buttons
19½" length ½"-diameter dowel
2 red beads with ½" opening to fit ends of dowel

Instructions

1. Cut 17½" x 45" piece of Wonder-Under. Press Wonder-Under onto wrong side of muslin piece. Remove paper backing. With short edges aligned and wrong sides facing, fold muslin in half. Fuse in place.

2. For dowel casing, referring to Diagram A, press fusible tape along raw edge and 5¼" in from raw edge on 1 side of muslin. Remove paper backing. Fold down edge 3"; fuse in place.

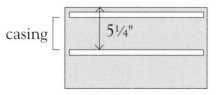

Diagram A

3. For pockets, cut 4 (12") lengths of fusible tape. Trim tape lengths to ½" wide. Referring to Diagram B, press fusible tape lengths onto front of muslin. Remove paper backing. Fold bottom edge up 6" and fuse in place.

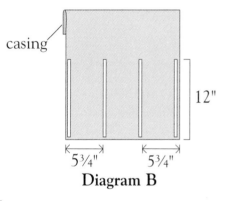

Diagram B

4. Using ruler and permanent black marker, draw stitching lines 6" in from each side of card holder on pockets.

5. Press Wonder-Under onto wrong side of appliqué fabrics, except fabrics to be used for gingerbread man, Christmas tree, and Santa. For "yuletide greetings" banner, from desired fabrics, cut 1 (3¾" x 14¼") piece for border, 4 (½") squares for corner blocks, and 1 (2¾" x 13¼") piece for center panel. For quilt block appliqués, from desired fabrics, cut 3 (3") squares for borders, 12 (½") squares for corner blocks, and 3 (2") squares for center blocks. Remove paper backing.

6. Referring to photo, center and fuse 3¾" x 14¼" border piece 1½" above pocket on front of card holder. Fuse corner blocks in place. Center and fuse 2¾" x 13¼" center panel in place.

7. Referring to photo, turn 3" border squares on point and fuse 1 square to center of each pocket. Fuse corner blocks in place on each border square. Turn 2" center block squares on

point. Center and fuse 1 block in place on each border square.

8. Trace patterns for gingerbread man, Christmas tree, and Santa on page 54 onto paper side of Wonder-Under. Leaving approximate ¼" margin, cut around shapes. Press shapes onto wrong side of fabrics (see photo for colors). Cut out shapes along pattern lines. Remove paper backing. Center and fuse shapes to quilt blocks

9. Use transfer paper to transfer "yuletide greetings" to center of 2¾" x 13¼" panel piece. Referring to photo, use permanent black marker to trace transferred words, to embellish appliqués with blanket stitches, and to draw eyes on Santa.

10. Hot-glue buttons to banner as desired. Insert dowel through casing. Hot-glue 1 bead to each end of dowel.

Santa Welcome Wreath

Let Santa wave his wand of holiday enchantment over all who enter your home. Simply fuse fabrics to posterboard to create this magical wreath.

Materials

Pellon® Wonder-Under® scraps
Fabric scraps for appliqués
8½" x 11" piece posterboard
Fine-tip permanent black fabric marker
Hot-glue gun and glue sticks
Twigs: 3 approximately 3" long,
    1 approximately 5" long
Greenery wreath
Artificial holly berries
Fabric bow

Instructions

1. Trace patterns onto paper side of Wonder-Under. Leaving approximate ½" margin, cut around shapes. Press shapes onto wrong side of fabric scraps. Cut out shapes along pattern lines.

2. Fuse shapes to posterboard in order indicated on patterns. Using permanent black marker, draw eyes. Cut out Santa, following outline of design. Cut out star shapes.

3. Referring to photo, hot-glue 1 small star to 1 end of each 3"-long twig. Hot-glue large star to 1 end of 5"-long twig. Hot-glue 5"-long twig in Santa's hand. Hot-glue 3"-long twigs behind Santa's pack.

4. Tuck artificial holly berries into wreath as desired. Hot-glue fabric bow to top of wreath and Santa to bottom of wreath.

How to Tie a Bow

If you would like to tie your own bow and would like to make one a little fancier than the one we show on our wreath, just follow these simple instructions.

For an 8"-wide bow, you will need 4 yards of ribbon and a 9" length of florist's wire. To make the bow, measure 4" from 1 end of the ribbon. Pinch the ribbon between your forefinger and thumb (this will be the center point of the bow). Make a 4" loop and pinch the ribbon again at the center (Diagram 1). Twist the ribbon one-half turn and make a loop on the opposite side. Make 5 loops on each side of the center in the same manner (Diagram 2). Fold the length of florist's wire over the center of the bow. Fold the bow in half across the wire. Holding the bow firmly, twist the wire ends together (Diagram 3). Fluff the bow by pulling firmly on the loops.

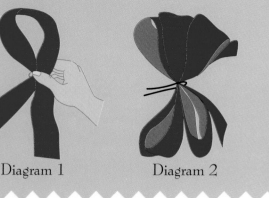

Diagram 1   Diagram 2   Diagram 3

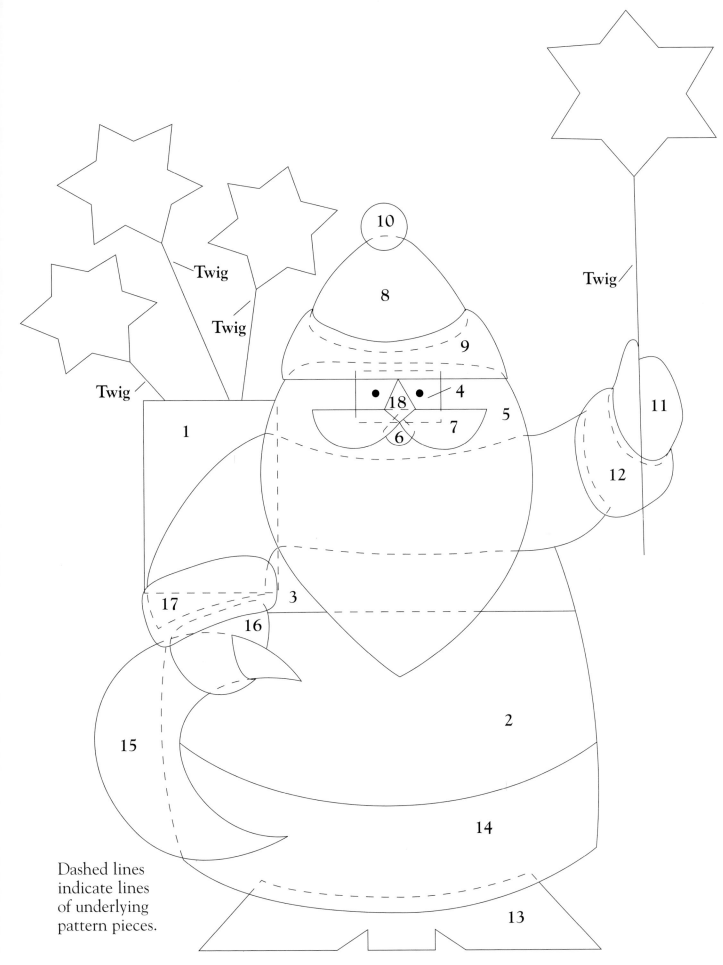

Twig

Twig

Twig

Twig

Twig

10

8

9

4

18

5

6

7

1

11

12

3

17

16

15

2

14

13

Dashed lines
indicate lines
of underlying
pattern pieces.

Package Tree Skirt

With this skirt you'll always find packages under your Christmas tree, even if Santa hasn't made his visit yet.

Materials

Felt: 50" square green for skirt, rectangles in variety of colors for packages
Fabric marking pencil
String
Thumbtack
Pellon® Heavy Duty Wonder-Under®
1 to 1½ yards each variety of ribbons
Liquid ravel preventer
Twist ties
Hot-glue gun and glue sticks
5½ yards of white jumbo rickrack

Instructions

1. To mark outer edge of tree skirt, fold 50" green felt square in half from top to bottom and then again from left to right. Use fabric marking pencil to mark center of square. Unfold felt once. Tie 1 end of string to fabric marking pencil. Insert thumbtack into string 24" from pencil. Referring to Diagram, insert thumbtack into felt at center point (A) and mark half-circle.

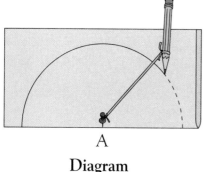

A

Diagram

2. To mark inner circle of tree skirt, repeat Step 1, inserting thumbtack into string 5" from pencil.

3. Cut out tree skirt along outer marked line. For back opening, cut straight from outer edge of tree skirt to inner circle. Then cut out inner circle along marked line.

4. Press Wonder-Under onto 1 side of each felt rectangle. Referring to photo, cut felt rectangles into desired sizes for packages. Do not remove paper backing.

5. For package ties, referring to photo for inspiration, measure width, length, or diagonal distance of each package. Cut pieces of ribbon equal to these measurements. Apply liquid ravel preventer to cut ends of ribbon pieces. Let dry. Cut strips of Wonder-Under equal to size of ribbon pieces. Press Wonder-Under strips to wrong side of corresponding ribbon pieces. Remove paper backing. Fuse ribbon pieces in place onto packages. Remove paper backing from packages.

6. Fuse felt packages as desired to 1 side of tree skirt. Using twist ties and remaining ribbon, tie bows. Hot-glue bows in place on packages. Hot-glue rickrack to outer edges and inner circle of tree skirt. Apply liquid ravel preventer to cut ends of rickrack. Let dry.

Evergreen Banner

This inviting scene adds just the right wintry touch to a corner of any room. Not only are the snowy forest appliqués no-sew, but so is the entire wall hanging!

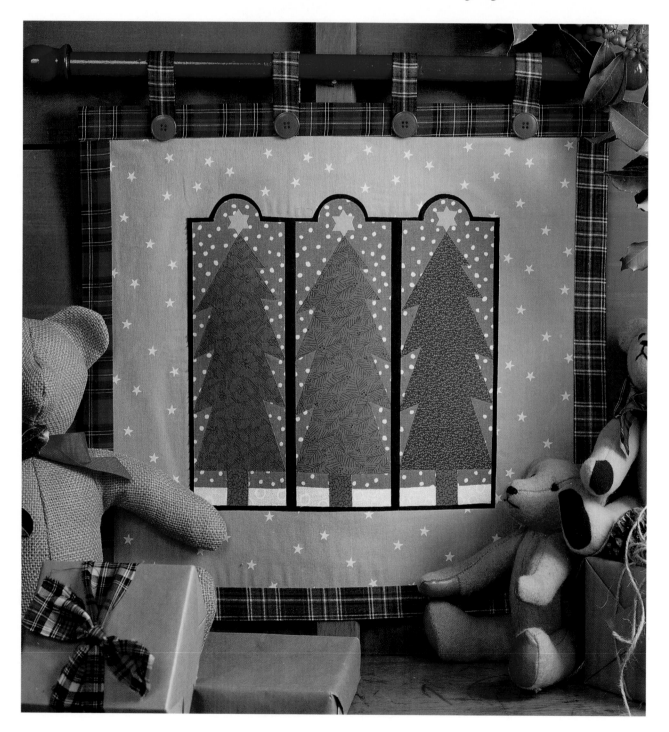

Materials

Pellon® Wonder-Under®
Fabrics: 2 (15" x 16") pieces tan;
    9" square dark blue; 8½" square
    light blue; scraps of white, brown,
    gold, and 3 different greens; 18" x
    20" piece red plaid
4 (¾") red buttons
Fabric glue
1"-diameter rod for hanging

Instructions

1. Cut 15" x 16" piece from Wonder-Under. Press Wonder-Under piece to wrong side of 1 tan fabric piece. Remove paper backing. With wrong sides facing and edges aligned, press tan fabric pieces together.

2. Trace appliqué patterns on page 62 onto paper side of Wonder-Under. Leaving approximate ½" margin, cut around shapes. Press design background onto wrong side of dark blue fabric, skies onto wrong side of light blue fabric, snows to wrong side of white fabric, tree trunks to wrong side of brown fabric, stars to wrong side of gold fabric, and 1 tree to wrong side of each green fabric. Cut out shapes along pattern lines. Remove paper backing.

3. Center and fuse dark blue design background on fused tan piece. Referring to photo, fuse remaining appliqués in place on dark blue design background in following order: skies, snows, tree trunks, trees, and stars.

4. For binding, cut following from red plaid: 2 (4" x 18") strips and 2 (4" x 17") strips. Fold 1" of each long edge of each red plaid strip to wrong side. (Long cut edges should meet at center of strip.) Press. Fold 1" of each short end of each strip to wrong side and press. From Wonder-Under, cut 2 (2" x 16") and 2 (2" x 15") strips. Press Wonder-Under strips onto wrong side of corresponding red plaid strips. Remove paper backing. Fold each strip in half lengthwise and finger-press.

5. Encase each side edge of tan piece in 1 folded 2" x 15" red plaid strip. Fuse side binding strips in place. Repeat to encase top and bottom edges in 2" x 16" binding strips.

6. For tabs, from red plaid, cut 4 (2" x 6") strips. Press each edge of each strip ½" onto wrong side. From Wonder-Under, cut 8 (1") squares. Press 1 Wonder-Under square onto wrong side of each end of each tab strip. Remove paper backing. Fold strip in half, with wrong sides facing. Referring to photo and spacing tabs evenly, slide top edge of wall hanging between layers of each tab. Fuse tabs in place.

7. Glue buttons to front of wall hanging on top of tabs. Let dry. Insert rod through tabs to hang.

Other Ideas

The long, skinny shape of an elegant evergreen lends itself well to a variety of rectangular projects. Fuse one of the trees down the left side of a purchased place mat or enlarge the pattern and fuse it to the center of a plain stocking.

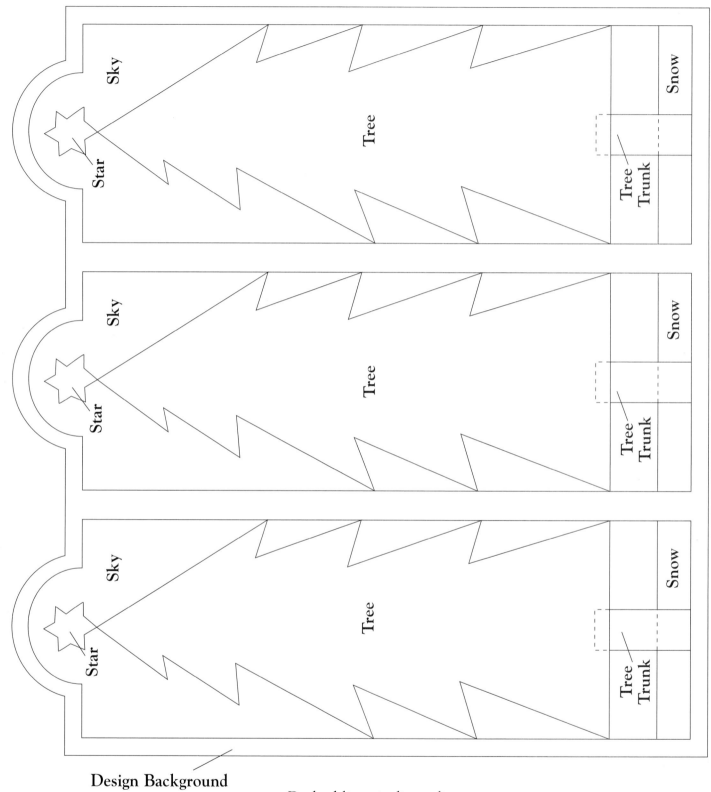

Design Background

Dashed lines indicate lines
of underlying pattern pieces.

Felt Ornaments

$\mathcal{T}$hese easy ornaments are a good parent-and-child project. Fuse the shapes together and let your children decorate and embellish the ornaments any way they choose.

Materials

For each:
Pellon® Heavy Duty Wonder-Under® scraps
10" length gold rope braid
Fabric glue

For gingerbread man:
5½" x 10" piece tan felt
White dimensional fabric paint in squeeze bottle
2 (½") black buttons
2 black seed beads

For star:
5" x 8" piece gold felt
Black dimensional fabric paint in squeeze bottle
½" buttons: 1 red, 1 white, 1 green

For stocking:
Felt: 2" x 8" piece red, 6" x 12" piece green, 2" square gold
Dimensional fabric paints in squeeze bottles: black, white
½" red button

Gingerbread Man Instructions

1. Trace gingerbread man shape on page 64 onto paper side of Wonder-Under. Leaving approximate ½" margin, cut around shape. Press shape onto wrong side of tan felt. Cut out shape

along pattern line. Remove paper backing. Trace gingerbread man shape again onto remainder of tan felt. Cut out shape along pattern lines.

2. With edges aligned and Wonder-Under to inside, stack gingerbread man shapes. Fold gold braid in half. Referring to photo, sandwich ½" of cut ends of gold braid between layers of gingerbread man at top of head. Fuse gingerbread man layers together, catching gold braid.

3. Referring to photo, use dimensional fabric paint to paint blanket stitches along edges of gingerbread man. Let dry. Glue buttons to center of gingerbread man. Glue seed beads in place for eyes. Let dry.

Star Instructions

1. Trace star shape onto paper side of Wonder-Under. Leaving approximate ½" margin, cut around shape. Press shape onto wrong side of gold felt. Cut out shape along pattern line. Remove paper backing. Trace star shape again onto remainder of gold felt. Cut out shape along pattern lines.

2. With edges aligned and Wonder-Under to inside, stack star shapes. Fold gold braid in half. Referring to photo, sandwich ½" of cut ends of gold braid between layers of star at top point. Fuse star layers together, catching gold braid.

3. Referring to photo, use dimensional fabric paint to paint blanket stitches along edges of star. Let dry. Glue buttons to center of star. Let dry.

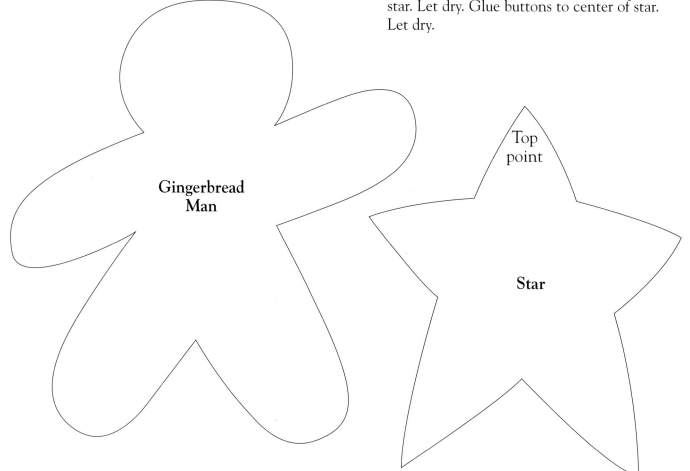

Gingerbread Man

Top point

Star

Stocking Instructions

1. Trace stocking, stocking cuff, and heart onto paper side of Wonder-Under. Leaving approximate ½" margin, cut around shapes. Press stocking cuff shape onto wrong side of red felt and stocking shape onto wrong side of green felt. Cut out shapes along pattern lines. Remove paper backing. Trace stocking cuff shape again onto remainder of red felt and stocking shape again to remainder of green felt. Cut out shapes along pattern lines.

2. With edges aligned and Wonder-Under to inside, stack stocking shapes. Fold gold braid in half. Referring to photo, sandwich ½" of cut ends of gold braid between layers of stocking at center top. Fuse stocking layers together, catching gold braid.

3. With edges of stocking cuff aligned and Wonder-Under to inside, stack stocking cuff shapes, sandwiching stocking between layers of stocking cuff and positioning so that top edge of stocking cuff is ¼" above top edge of stocking. Fuse stocking cuff layers together, catching stocking between.

4. Referring to photo, use black dimensional fabric paint to paint blanket stitches along edges of stocking. Let dry. Use white dimensional fabric paint to paint blanket stitches along edges of stocking cuff. Let dry. Trace heart pattern onto gold felt. Cut out heart along pattern line. Glue heart to center of stocking. Glue button to center of heart. Let dry.

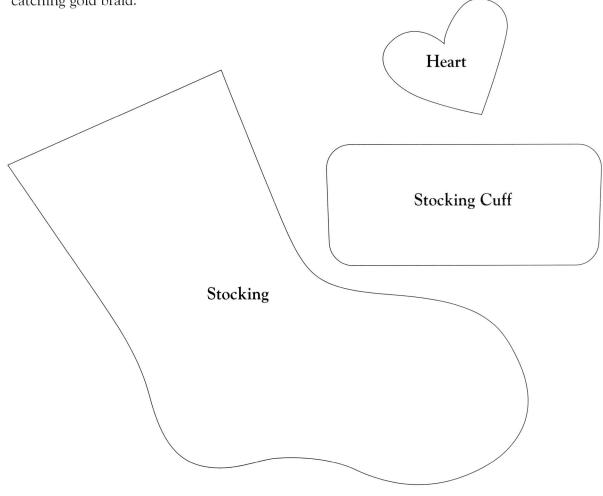

Heart

Stocking Cuff

Stocking

Merry Muslin Stockings

These stockings, decorated with patches and appliqués, bring the warmth of a country Christmas to your hearth. A quick-and-easy project, they are ideal for treats and lightweight treasures.

Materials (for 1 stocking)

2 (12" x 16") pieces heavyweight
   muslin
Straight pins
Pinking shears
Fabric glue
Pellon® Heavy Duty Wonder-Under®
Fabrics: scraps for appliqués, 4" x 6"
   strip for hanger
¾"-wide Pellon® Heavy Duty Wonder-
   Under® fusible tape
Hot-glue gun and glue sticks
1⅛" button
Fine-tip permanent black fabric marker

Instructions

1. Trace stocking patterns on page 68 onto right side of 1 muslin piece. With wrong sides facing, pin muslin pieces together. Cutting through both layers with pinking shears, cut out stocking along pattern lines.

2. Apply line of fabric glue along side and bottom edges on wrong side of stocking back. Stack stocking front on top of stocking back, aligning edges. Press lightly along glued edges. Let dry flat.

3. Trace heel and toe patterns onto paper side of Wonder-Under; then trace either gingerbread man and heart patterns at right or tree and star patterns on page 68. Leaving approximate ½" margin, cut around shapes. Press shapes onto wrong side of appliqué fabrics.

Cut out shapes along pattern lines. Remove paper backing. Referring to photo, arrange appliqués on stocking front. Fuse in place.

4. For hanger, fold 1" of each long edge of fabric strip to wrong side. (Long cut edges should meet at center of strip.) Press. Fold 1" of each short end of strip to wrong side and press. Press fusible tape along each long pressed edge. Remove paper backing. Fold strip in half lengthwise and fuse. With short ends aligned, fold strip in half. Hot-glue ends together. Then hot-glue approximately 1" of ends of hanger to top left corner on front of stocking.

5. Hot-glue button over ends of hanger. Referring to photo, use permanent black marker to draw blanket stitches on appliqués.

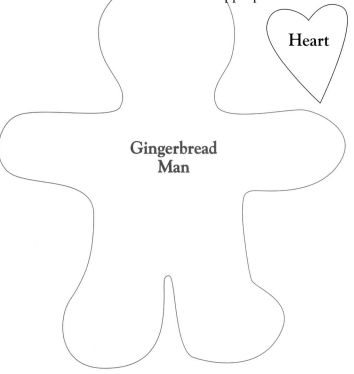

Heart

Gingerbread
Man

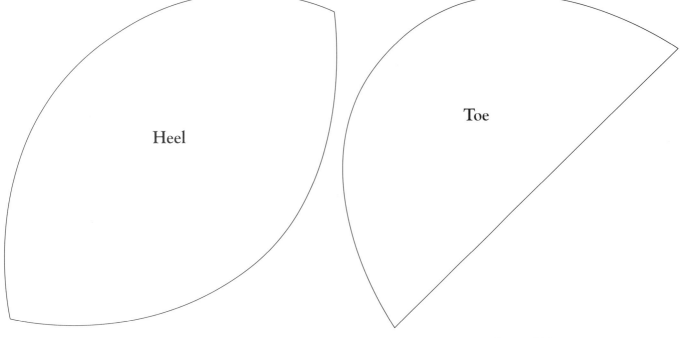

Heel

Toe

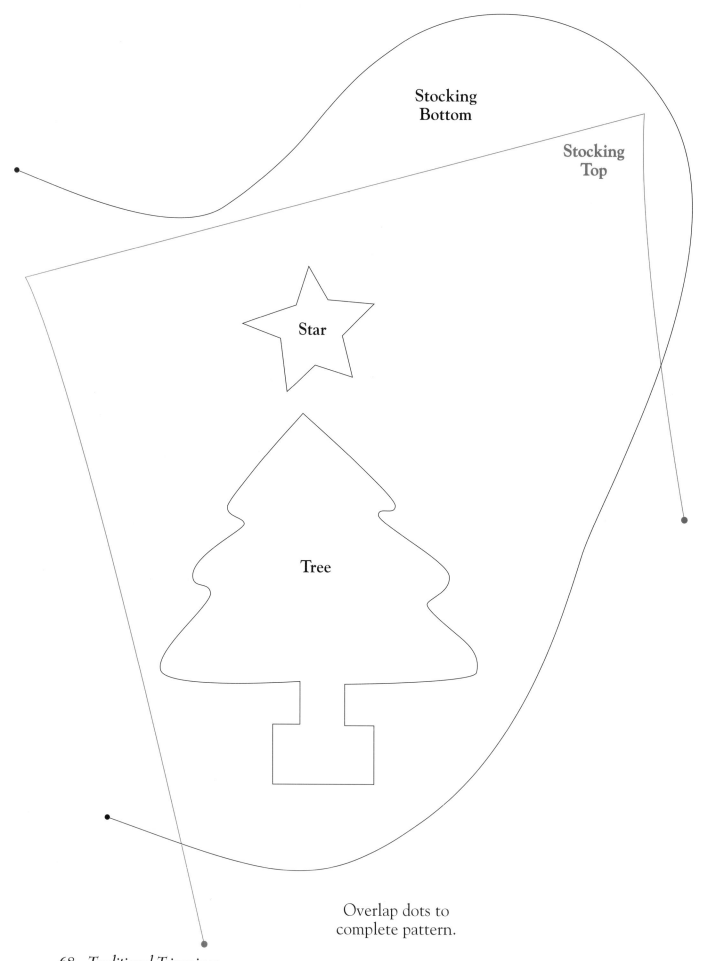

Stocking
Bottom

Stocking
Top

Star

Tree

Overlap dots to
complete pattern.

Opulence
Under the Tree

𝒯his tree skirt immediately suggests elegance and sophistication.
Fabrics such as damask and brocade, along with gold braid
and tassels, enhance the refined look.

Materials

Fabrics: 55" square medium- to heavy-weight solid for skirt, ½ yard 44"-wide striped for scallops

Fabric marking pencil

String

Thumbtack

Yardstick

¼"-wide double-fold bias tape to match fabrics

Fabric glue

¾"-wide Pellon® Heavy Duty Wonder-Under® fusible tape

Transparent tape

3¼ yards ¼"-wide decorative braid

Hot-glue gun and glue sticks

5¼ yards ½"-diameter twisted cording

1¼ yards ¼"-wide flat gold braid

5 (5"-long) tassels

Instructions

1. With right sides facing, fold solid-colored fabric square in half from top to bottom and then again from left to right. Use fabric marking pencil to mark center of square. Unfold fabric once.

2. To mark outer guideline, tie 1 end of string to fabric marking pencil. Measure and mark string 26½" from pencil; insert thumbtack into string at this point. Referring to Diagram A, insert thumbtack into fabric at center point (A) and mark half-circle.

3. Referring to Diagram B, insert thumbtack into fabric at 1 edge of drawn half-circle (B) and mark quarter-circle. Repeat, placing thumbtack at opposite edge of half-circle (C).

4. To mark inner cutting line, repeat Step 2, inserting thumbtack into string 1¼" from pencil.

5. To mark outer cutting line, refer to Diagram C and use yardstick and fabric marking pencil to draw 3 sides of hexagon. Cutting through both fabric layers, cut out inner circle and hexagon. For opening in back of skirt, cut fabric along 1 fold from outer edge to inner circle.

6. To cover raw edge of inner circle, encase edge in fold of bias tape, trimming tape to fit. Use fabric glue to secure. Let dry.

7. To fuse skirt, press fusible tape to wrong side along outer edges of skirt. Remove paper backing. Fold edge to wrong side along inner edge of tape. Fuse in place. Repeat to hem opening edges.

8. For scallop, make complete pattern by matching dots and taping top and bottom pattern pieces together. Matching arrows on pattern to stripes on fabric and leaving at least ½" between scallops, transfer 6 scallops to wrong side of striped fabric.

9. To attach each scallop to skirt, press fusible tape along each straight edge of scallop. Remove paper backing. Referring to photo, center 1 scallop along 1 straight edge of skirt, with curved part of scallop extending beyond edge of skirt. Fuse in place. Repeat for remaining scallops.

10. To prevent ends of braid or cording from fraying after cutting, apply fabric glue to ½" of area to be cut. Let dry and then cut. Hot-glue ¼"-wide decorative braid along straight edges of each scallop.

11. Beginning at skirt opening, hot-glue cording along edges of skirt, extending cording at each hexagon point to form a 2"-long loop. Secure each loop by wrapping a 4" length of flat braid around base of loop. Hot-glue to secure. Hot-glue 1 tassel to each loop. Wrap a 4" length of flat braid around each tassel. Hot-glue to secure.

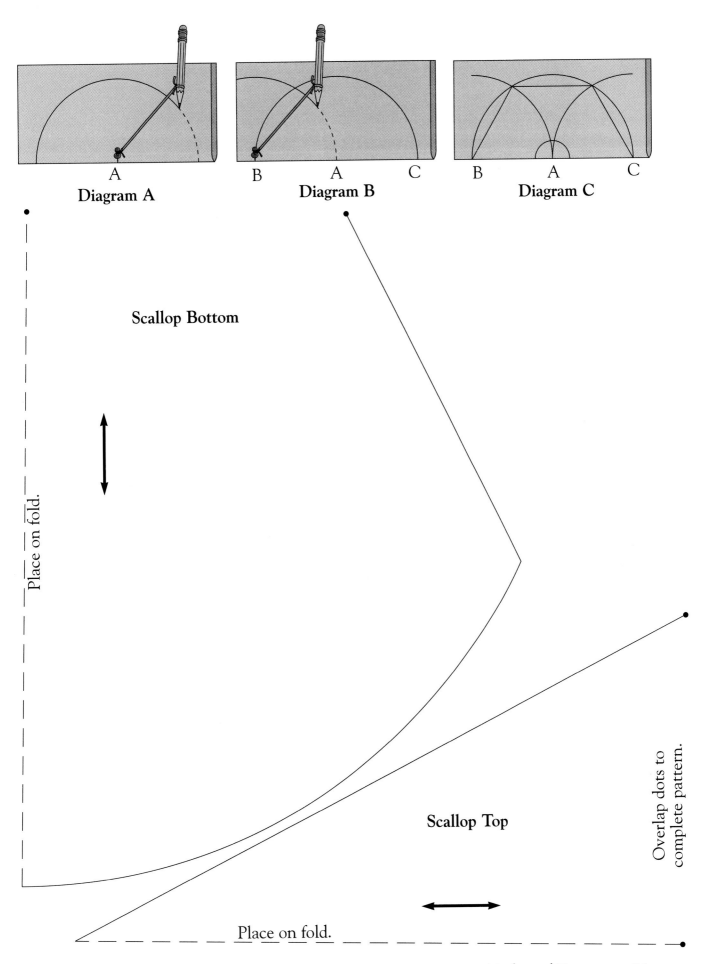

A

Diagram A

B A C

Diagram B

B A C

Diagram C

Scallop Bottom

Place on fold.

Scallop Top

Place on fold.

Overlap dots to complete pattern.

Saint Nick Ornament

$\mathcal{F}$use fabrics to a piece of batting to create this merry ornament. Colored-pencil shading and patterned fabrics give Santa detail and dimension. Use a fine-tip marker to "stitch" the edges.

Materials

Pellon® Wonder-Under® scraps
Fabric scraps for hat, hat trim, eyebrows, mustache, beard, and star appliqués
Muslin scrap for face appliqué
Small sharp scissors
5" square of low-loft cotton batting
Colored pencils: dark pink, peach, brown
Fine-tip permanent fabric markers: black, brown
Wooden star cutout
Hot-glue gun and glue sticks
9" length of jute twine

Instructions

1. Trace hat, hat trim, eyebrows, face, mustache, and beard shapes onto paper side of Wonder-Under. Leaving approximate ¼" margin, cut around shapes. Referring to photo for colors, press shapes onto wrong side of fabric scraps. Cut out shapes along pattern lines. Remove paper backing.

2. Place face piece right side up on pattern and use a regular pencil to trace features. Make small clips in face piece between nose and cheeks as indicated by blue lines on pattern.

3. Referring to photo, arrange appliqués at center of batting square in order indicated on patterns, overlapping clipped area of nose over mustache. Fuse in place.

4. Leaving approximate ⅛" of margin outside appliqués, cut Santa from batting.

5. Referring to photo, use dark pink and peach pencils to shade cheeks and nose and brown pencil to shade nose. Use black permanent fabric marker to draw over pencil lines on face and to outline nose. Use brown permanent fabric marker to outline mustache and to draw stitching lines along edges of beard and hat trim.

6. Using wooden star as pattern, transfer star shape to Wonder-Under side of star fabric. Cut out shape along pattern lines. Remove paper backing. Fuse fabric star shape onto wooden star. Referring to photo, hot-glue star onto Santa.

7. For hanger, knot ends of twine together. Glue knot to top back of Santa.

Fusible Fact

Any printed material or traceable object is a potential pattern. Children's books, coloring books, rubber stamps, greeting cards, and wrapping paper are great pattern sources. (Keep in mind, though, that copyright laws prohibit using someone else's design on something you sell or make in quantity, unless you get written permission from the copyright holder.)

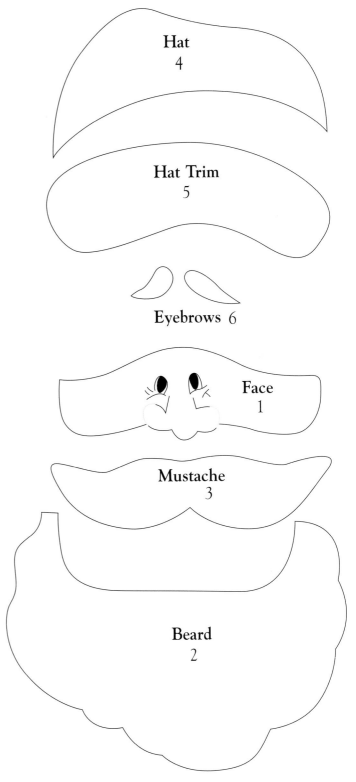

Hat
4

Hat Trim
5

Eyebrows 6

Face
1

Mustache
3

Beard
2

Countdown
to
Christmas

1 2
3 4
5 6
7 8
9 10
11 12
13 14
15 16
17 18
19 20
21 22
23 24

Candy Countdown Calendar

$\mathcal{W}$hat a delicious way to await Christmas! Simply unwrap a piece of candy each day in December, and by the time you have eaten all of the tasty treats, Christmas will have arrived!

Materials

- ¾"-wide Pellon® Heavy Duty Wonder-Under® fusible tape
- 7" x 49" piece white felt
- 3⅓ yards ⅞"-wide plaid ribbon
- Yardstick
- Disappearing-ink fabric marker
- Green paint pen
- 5⅓ yards ⅛"-wide green satin ribbon
- 24 small safety pins
- 24 peppermint candies in cellophane wrappers
- 8" bellpull rod
- 1½ yards red satin cording

Instructions

1. Press fusible tape along 1 short edge of white felt piece. Remove paper backing. Fold edge down 3" and fuse in place to form casing.

2. Press fusible tape onto wrong side of plaid ribbon. Remove paper backing. On front of felt piece, use yardstick and disappearing-ink fabric marker to measure and mark 7" down from top edge. Align bottom edge of plaid ribbon with this mark. Fuse ribbon across width of felt piece, trimming ribbon as necessary. In same manner, fuse ribbon to top, bottom, and sides of entire felt piece, mitering corners.

3. Using fabric marker, lightly draw line 2½" from each side along entire length of felt piece. (You will use these lines for centering numbers.)

4. To position numbers, on left-hand line, use fabric marker to mark 8" from top edge of felt piece. Continue making marks along this line in 3" increments. On right-hand line, mark 9" from top edge of felt piece. Continue making marks along this line in 3" increments.

5. Referring to photo and using fabric marker, write numbers 1 through 24 at marks (numbers should be approximately 1" tall, and base of numbers should rest on marks); write "Countdown to Christmas" in top block. Using paint pen, paint over numbers and words. Let dry.

6. Cut satin ribbon into 24 (8") lengths. Using fabric marker, mark ⅜" below each number on centering lines. Working from back of felt piece, center and pin 1 satin ribbon length to front of felt piece at each mark. Tie each ribbon length in bow around 1 end of candy wrapper. Carefully remove all fabric marker lines.

7. Insert bellpull rod through casing. Tie satin cording to each end of rod, trimming cording to desired length. Knot ends of cording.

Wooden Spoon Angels

Any cook would love an ornament made from a favorite kitchen utensil.
These are a great way to spoon up some holiday cheer.

Materials (for 3 angels)

Wooden spoons: 1 each small, medium, and large
Dimensional paints in squeeze bottle: blue, pink
51" yellow rickrack
Liquid ravel preventer
Fabric glue
Pellon® Wonder-Under®
Fabrics: 10" x 14" piece blue polka-dot, 9" x 10" piece pink polka-dot
Purchased appliqués: 2 yellow stars, 1 white heart
3 (9"-diameter) cotton lace doilies
3 (10") lengths of gold metallic thread

Instructions

1. Referring to photo, paint face on bowl of each spoon, using blue for eyes and pink for mouth. Let dry. Cut rickrack into 6 (8½") lengths. Apply liquid ravel preventer to cut ends of rickrack. Let dry. Referring to photo, glue 2 lengths of rickrack around bowl of each spoon for hair. Let dry.

2. Trace 2 of each body pattern onto paper side of Wonder-Under. Leaving approximate ½" margin, cut around shapes. Press small and medium body shapes onto wrong side of blue fabric. Press large body shape onto wrong side of pink fabric. Remove paper backing.

3. With wrong sides facing and raw edges aligned, fuse matching body pieces together. Referring to photo, glue 1 star appliqué to 1 side of each blue body and heart appliqué to 1 side of pink body. Let dry.

4. With wrong sides facing, fold each doily in half and glue. Let dry. Referring to photo, stack 1 doily, large spoon (right side up and centered on doily), and pink body (right side up and centered on spoon). Glue layers together to secure. Let dry. Repeat, using blue bodies, to assemble medium and small angels.

5. For each hanger, fold 1 length of gold metallic thread in half. Glue ends to back of 1 head. Let dry.

Body

Cutting line for small body

Cutting line for medium body

Cutting line for large body

Glorious Gifts

The pages of this chapter contain a sleighful of suggestions for all of your holiday gift-giving needs. You'll want to start decorating Christmas tins, pillowcases, tote bags, button covers, and much, much more!

Page 93

Page 98

Page 82

Page 96

Christmas Treat Bags

These little bags make terrific party favors when filled with sweet surprises. They're quick to make, using brown lunch sacks and fabric cutouts. The messages and "stitching" are drawn on with black markers.

Materials (for 1 bag)

Pellon® Wonder-Under®
Fabrics for appliqués
Brown lunch sack
Fine-tip permanent black marker
Medium-tip permanent black marker
   (optional, for message)
28" length raffia
Hot-glue gun and glue sticks
Tissue paper

Instructions

Note: Use a dry iron for this project. No press cloth is needed.

1. Trace desired appliqué shapes onto paper side of Wonder-Under. Leaving approximate ½" margin, cut around shapes. Referring to photo for colors, press shapes onto wrong side of appliqué fabrics. Cut out shapes along pattern lines. Remove paper backing.

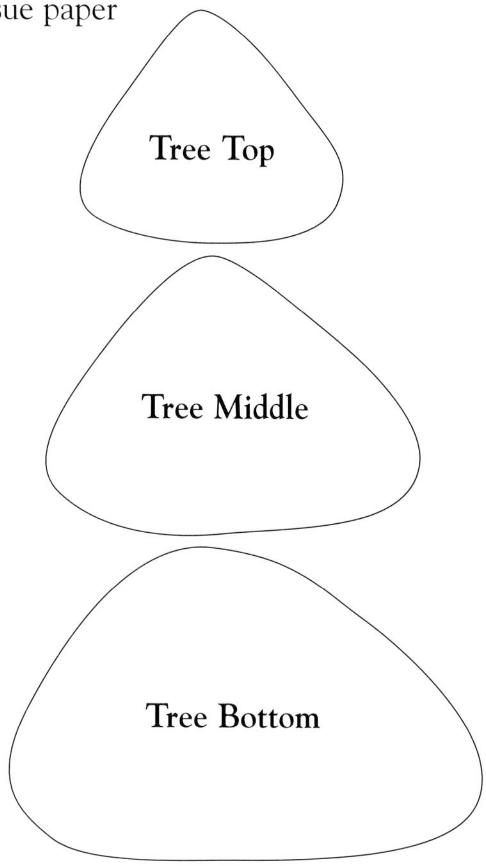

Tree Top

Tree Middle

Tree Bottom

Tree Trunk

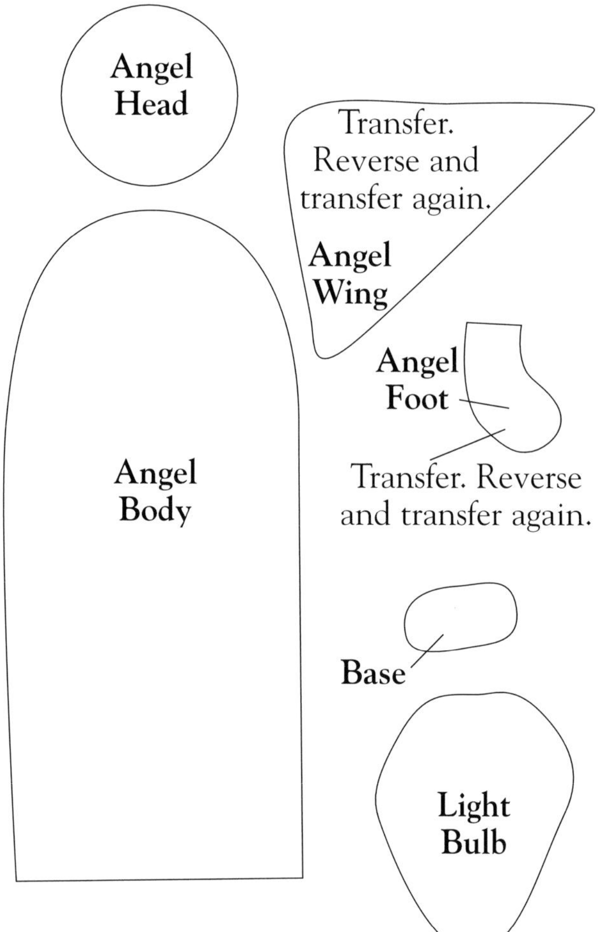

Angel Head

Angel Body

Transfer. Reverse and transfer again.

Angel Wing

Angel Foot

Transfer. Reverse and transfer again.

Base

Light Bulb

2. With bag flat, arrange shapes on front of bag, overlapping pieces if necessary. Fuse shapes in place.

3. Referring to photo and using fine-tip marker, embellish appliqués with pen stitching. If desired, use medium-point marker to write message on bag.

4. Tie raffia in bow and then trim ends. Hot-glue bow to top of bag. Line bag with tissue paper.

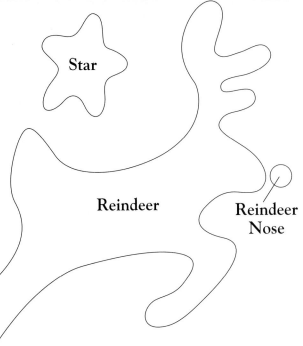

Star

Reindeer

Reindeer
Nose

Holly-day Pillowcases

Seasonal linens make a wonderful hostess gift. Purchase inexpensive pillowcases and then fuse this classic Christmas motif along the edges. Accent with buttons and dimensional paint.

Materials (for 1 pair of pillowcases)

⅛ yard green fabric
2 purchased cotton pillowcases
¼ yard Pellon® Wonder-Under®
Green dimensional fabric paint in squeeze bottle
18 (½") red buttons
Washable acrylic jewel fabric glue

Instructions

1. Wash, dry, and iron pillowcases and fabric. Do not use fabric softener in washer or dryer.

2. Trace holly leaf pattern 18 times onto paper side of Wonder-Under. Leaving approximate ½" margin, cut around shapes. Press shapes onto wrong side of green fabric. Cut out shapes along pattern lines. Remove paper backing.

3. Referring to photo, position 3 sets of 3 holly leaves each along front open edge of each pillowcase. Fuse holly leaves in place.

4. Using dimensional paint, outline holly leaves and draw vein in center of each leaf. Let dry.

5. Referring to photo, glue 3 buttons in place at base of each set of holly leaves. Let dry.

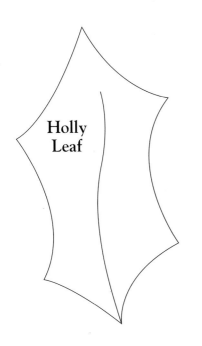

Holly Leaf

Other Ideas

Appliqué an entire holly-day gift set. Create the pillowcases and then fuse the motif to the hem of guest towels and to the center of a plain throw pillow. The ensemble will quickly transform a guest room into a holiday haven for out-of-town company.

Christmas-Card Bookmarks

*H*ere's a great way to recycle old Christmas cards. Select an elegant card for your grandmother or a whimsical one for a child.

Materials (for 1 bookmark)

Pellon® Wonder-Under®
Front of old Christmas card
Scissors: regular or decorative-blade
Colored card stock
Decorative hole punch (optional)
Permanent markers in variety of colors
    or gold paint pen (optional)
Iron-on matte finish vinyl

Instructions

Note: Use a dry iron and dry press cloth for this project.

1. Press Wonder-Under onto wrong side of Christmas card front. Cut out desired shape and size motif from Christmas card front, using regular or decorative-blade scissors.

2. Arrange Christmas card motif on card stock. Use regular or decorative-blade scissors to cut card stock in desired size needed for bookmark background.

3. Remove paper backing from motif. Fuse motif onto front of card-stock shape.

4. If desired, use decorative hole punch to embellish bookmark; use markers or paint pen to draw details or write message onto bookmark.

5. Cut out vinyl pieces for front and back of bookmark, leaving approximate ½" margin of vinyl along each edge. Remove backing from vinyl. Apply vinyl to front and back of bookmark. Smooth out any bubbles and trim edges. Referring to manufacturer's instructions, iron vinyl.

Stained-glass Tin

Package your favorite colorful candies in this brilliant lamé tin.
The metallic shine of the fabric and the black dimensional
paint create the sparkling stained-glass look.

Materials

Tin (at least 7½" square) with lid
Spray paints: gold, white
Lamé fabrics: 6" square red, 4" x 7"
    piece green, 8" square gold
4" x 7" piece white fabric
Lightweight fusible interfacing
Pellon® Wonder-Under®
6¼" square medium-weight cardboard
Disappearing-ink fabric marker
Black dimensional fabric paint in
    squeeze bottle
Batting
Craft glue
1 yard ¼"-diameter red metallic
    twisted cording
Hot-glue gun and glue sticks

Instructions

1. Spray-paint outside of tin base gold. Let dry. Spray-paint outside of tin lid white. Let dry. Set tin aside.

2. Fuse interfacing to wrong side of red lamé, green lamé, and white fabric.

3. Trace berry and flame patterns onto paper side of Wonder-Under 3 times each. Then trace leaf cluster pattern onto paper side of Wonder-Under; reverse pattern and transfer once more. Draw 1 (1¼" x 3") rectangle and 2 (1¼" x 2½") rectangles on paper side of Wonder-Under. Leaving approximate ½" margin, cut around shapes.

4. Press berry and flame shapes onto wrong side of red lamé, leaf cluster shapes onto wrong side of green lamé, and rectangles onto wrong side of white fabric. Cut out shapes along pattern lines. Remove paper backing.

5. Round off corners of cardboard square. Center cardboard on right side of gold lamé. Using disappearing-ink fabric marker, draw around cardboard square. Remove cardboard.

6. Referring to photo, position rectangle candles, flames, leaf clusters, and berries in drawn square on gold lamé. Fuse in place.

7. Referring to photo, use dimensional fabric paint to cover raw edges of appliqués, to paint detail lines, and to cover fabric marker line. Let dry.

8. Cut 2 (6¼") squares of batting. To form padded shape, place gold lamé decorated side down onto flat surface. Center both squares of batting and then cardboard on gold lamé. Alternating sides and pulling fabric taut, use craft glue to glue edges of fabric to back of cardboard. Let dry.

9. Hot-glue padded shape to top of tin lid. With center of cording at center top of shape, hot-glue cording around shape. Tie ends of cording in knot. Knot each streamer 1" from ends and then fray ends.

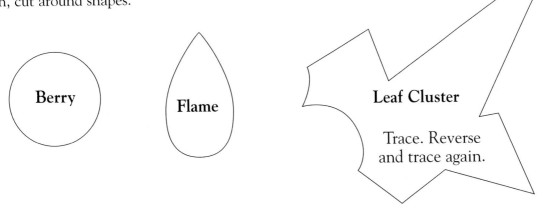

Berry

Flame

Leaf Cluster

Trace. Reverse
and trace again.

Textured Tidings

$\mathscr{P}$ress Pellon® Wonder-Under® onto scraps of Christmas fabrics, cut out various ornament shapes, add a little dimensional paint, and—voilà—you have custom-made greeting cards in no time!

Materials (for 1 card)

- Pellon® Wonder-Under® scraps
- Christmas fabric scrap
- Blank greeting card with matching envelope
- Dimensional paints in squeeze bottles: gold glitter, variety of colors to coordinate with fabric
- ⅛"-wide satin ribbon scraps
- Fabric glue

Instructions

Note: Use a dry iron for this project. No press cloth is needed.

1. Trace desired ornament outline on page 90 onto paper side of Wonder-Under. Leaving approximate ½" margin, cut around shape. Press ornament shape onto wrong side of fabric. Cut out shape along pattern line. (For Ornament A, also cut out center tree motif.) Remove paper backing.

2. Fuse ornament onto front of blank greeting card.

3. Referring to photo and pattern, use gold glitter dimensional paint to draw ornament cap. Let dry. Outline raw edges of ornaments and add details, using coordinating dimensional paints (see photo). Let dry.

4. For hanger for Ornament A, referring to photo, glue satin ribbon length from top of card to top of ornament cap. Tie remaining ribbon in bow and trim ends. Glue bow in place at top of ornament cap. Let dry.

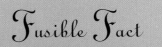

Fusible Fact

For paper projects such as this one where a dry iron is used, no press cloth is needed. However, if you want to be sure to avoid getting adhesive on your iron, you can use a *dry* press cloth. Brown paper bags—or transparent silicone-treated pressing paper available at crafts stores—make good dry press cloths. You can also use scraps of Wonder-Under release paper from which the web has been removed.

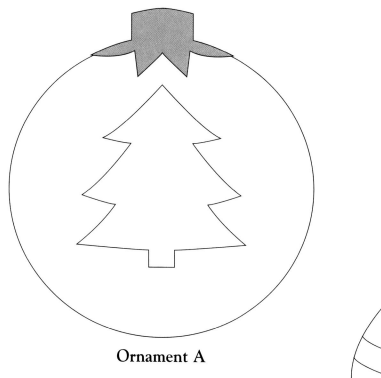

Ornament A

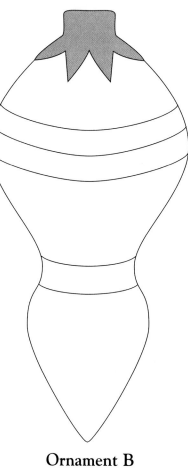

Ornament B

Candy-Cane Baby Bib

These candy canes are guaranteed not to make a sticky mess! In fact, they will help keep your baby clean for all of those holiday hugs.

Materials

Plain purchased bib
8½" x 10" piece red-and-white
   striped fabric
Pellon® Wonder-Under®
Silver fabric paint pen
½ yard ½"-wide green ribbon
1 (10-mm) gold jingle bell
1 safety pin

Instructions

1. Wash, dry, and iron bib and fabric. Do not use fabric softener in washer or dryer.

2. Trace pattern onto paper side of Wonder-Under. Reverse pattern and trace again. Leaving approximate ½" margin, cut around shapes. Press shapes onto wrong side of red-and-white striped fabric, positioning shapes on bias. Cut out shapes along pattern lines. Remove paper backing.

3. Referring to photo, crisscross candy canes and center on front of bib. Fuse candy canes in place.

4. Outline candy canes with silver paint pen. Let dry.

5. Thread ribbon through top of jingle bell and tie in bow. Trim ends of ribbon to desired length. Referring to photo, position bow on front of bib at intersection of candy canes. Working from back of bib, pin bow in place. Unpin and remove bow before laundering bib.

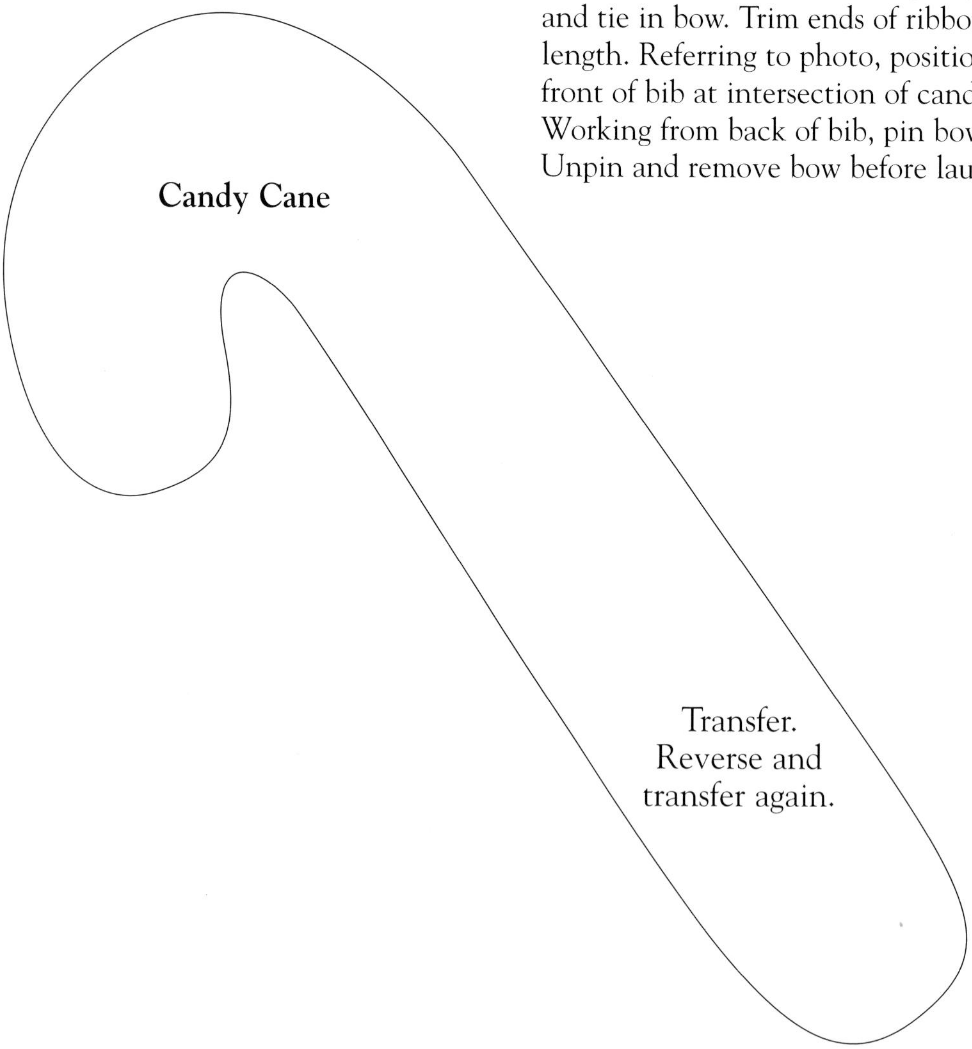

Candy Cane

Transfer.
Reverse and
transfer again.

Happy Holiday Tote

This handy bag is ideal for transporting an armload of Christmas packages.

Materials

- ¾"-wide Pellon® Heavy Duty Wonder-Under® fusible tape
- 2 yards 1½"-wide plaid ribbon
- Purchased tote bag
- Pellon® Heavy Duty Wonder-Under®
- Fabric scraps: white, blue, red-and-white striped, green, yellow
- Fabric paint pens: brown, orange, black
- White dimensional fabric paint in squeeze bottle

Instructions

1. Press fusible tape onto wrong side of ribbon. Remove paper backing. Referring to photo, fuse ribbon to 1 side of bag, mitering corners.

2. Trace 1 snowman, 1 snow woman, 1 scarf, 1 apron, 1 top hat, 1 sun hat, 1 man's outside hand, 1 man's inside hand, 1 woman's hand, 2 trees, and 4 stars onto paper side of Wonder-Under. Leaving approximate ¼" margin, cut around shapes. Referring to photo for colors, press shapes onto wrong side of fabrics. Cut out shapes along pattern lines.

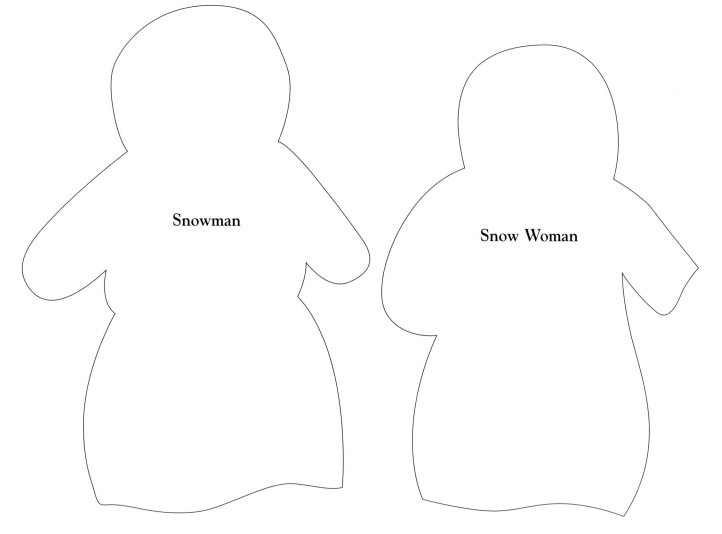

Snowman

Snow Woman

3. Remove paper backing from scarf and apron. Referring to photo, fuse scarf onto snowman and apron onto snow woman. Remove paper backing from snowman, snow woman, and remaining shapes. Referring to photo, fuse shapes in place on front of tote.

4. Referring to photo, use brown paint pen to draw hair on snow woman. Let dry. Use orange paint pen to draw carrot noses on snowman and snow woman. Let dry. Use black paint pen to draw facial details and blanket stitching along edges of shapes. Let dry. Use white dimensional fabric paint to paint snow lines on ground and to paint snowflakes dots in sky. Let dry.

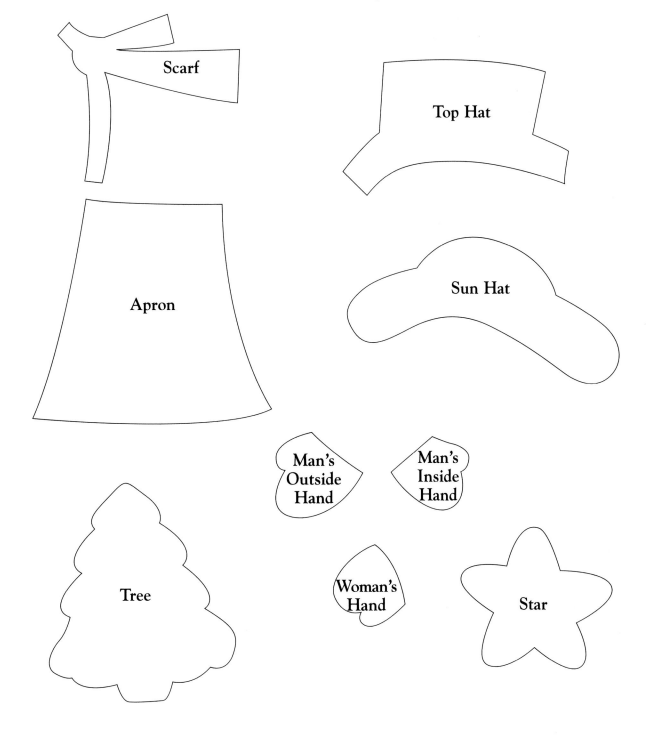

Evergreen Goody Boxes

Dressed up with a forest of appliqués, these fabric-covered Shaker boxes make festive containers for tasty holiday treats.

Materials (for 1 box)

Spray paint in color to match fabric
Shaker box
Design Master® glossy wood-tone
    spray *
Pellon® Heavy Duty Wonder-Under®
Fabrics to cover box lid and for
    appliqués
Pellon® Fusible Fleece
Ribbon to cover side of box lid
Craft glue
Spring-type clothespins
Dimensional fabric paints in squeeze
    bottles in colors to match fabrics
* Available at crafts stores

Instructions

Note: Use a dry iron and press cloth for this project.

1. Spray-paint outside of box base. Let dry. Lightly spray outside of box base with wood-tone spray. Let dry. Press Wonder-Under onto wrong side of all background fabrics.

2. To cover box lid with 1 background fabric, place lid upside down on wrong side of desired background fabric. Draw around lid. Cut out fabric ½" outside drawn line. At ½" intervals, clip edge of fabric to within ⅛" of line. Remove paper backing.

3. Use lid again as pattern to cut piece of fleece in same size as lid. Fuse fleece to top of lid. Let dry. Center background fabric piece right side up on top of lid. Fuse fabric to lid and to sides of lid. If necessary, trim edges of fabric even with bottom edge of lid.

4. To cover lid with 2 background fabrics, repeat steps 2 and 3. Then, referring to photo, cut a second fabric piece in desired size to cover part of lid, allowing ½" allowance on all

sides for finishing. Remove paper backing. Press top edge of fabric piece ½" to wrong side, being careful not to let iron touch exposed Wonder-Under. Position fabric piece faceup on fabric-covered lid as desired. Fuse fabric piece in place. Clip side edges and then fuse side edges to sides of lid as in Step 3. Glue pressed edge in place. Let dry.

5. Trace star, tree, and trunk patterns desired number of times onto paper side of Wonder-Under. Leaving approximate ½" margin, cut around shapes. Referring to photo for colors, press shapes onto wrong side of appliqué fabrics. Cut out shapes along pattern lines. Remove paper backing. Arrange appliqués on top of fabric-covered lid, overlapping appliqués as necessary. Fuse in place.

6. Measure around side of lid and add ½" to this measurement. Cut length of ribbon to determined measurement. Glue ribbon to side of lid, securing with clothespins until glue is dry.

7. Use dimensional fabric paints to paint dots on trees and to paint dots along center of ribbon on side of lid. Let dry.

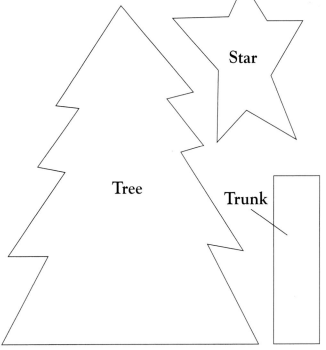

Star

Tree

Trunk

Merry Mittens

A pair of jolly ol' mittens keeps little fingers warm
during the holiday season.

Materials

Pellon® Heavy Duty Wonder-Under®
4" x 6½" piece white plush felt
Felt scraps: pink, red
1 pair purchased red mittens
Flexible fabric glue
4 (10-mm) wiggle eyes
2 (1"-diameter) white pom-poms

Instructions

Note: It may be necessary to adjust pattern to
fit mittens. If so, enlarge or reduce patterns
using photocopier.

1. Trace beard and face patterns onto paper
side of Wonder-Under 2 times each. Mark on
beards where face area will be placed. Leaving
approximate ½" margin, cut around shapes.
Press beard shapes onto wrong side of white
plush felt. Press face shapes onto wrong side
of pink felt. Cut out shapes along pattern lines.
Cut out face area from center of each beard.
Remove paper backing.

2. Referring to photo, fuse 1 face piece onto
center back of each mitten. Fuse 1 beard
around each face piece.

3. For noses, cut out 2 (⅜"-diameter) circles
from red felt. Using fabric glue, glue 1 nose to
each face piece. Glue 2 wiggle eyes to each
face piece. Glue 1 pom-pom to center top of
each mitten.

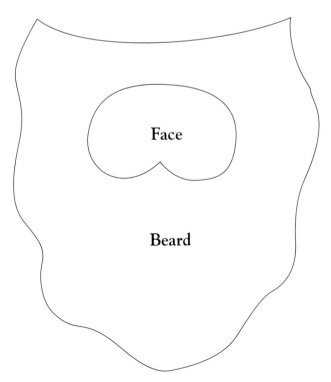

Face

Beard

Christmas-Lights Button Covers

*L*ight up a friend's holiday wardrobe with these bright button covers. Because the lights are made by fusing layers of fabric together, they are a very inexpensive gift.

Materials (for 4 button covers)

Pellon® Heavy Duty Wonder-Under®
Fabrics: 1 (5" x 7") piece yellow;
    2 (5" x 7") pieces white; 1 (4")
    square each red, green, and blue
Glossy black paint pen
Hot-glue gun and glue sticks
4 button covers

Instructions

1. Cut 2 (5" x 7") pieces from Wonder-Under. With edges aligned, press 1 Wonder-Under piece onto wrong side of yellow fabric. Remove paper backing. Aligning edges, fuse 1 white fabric piece on top of yellow fabric and then press remaining 5" x 7" Wonder-Under piece on top of white side of fused yellow-and-white fabric piece. Remove paper backing. Align edges and fuse remaining white fabric piece on top of yellow-and-white fabric piece.

2. Cut 5 (2") squares from fused yellow-and-white fabric. Cut 4 (2") squares each from red, green, and blue fabrics. Cut 12 (2") squares from Wonder-Under. Fuse red squares together as in Step 1, ending with layer of Wonder-Under. Do *not* remove paper backing from final layer of Wonder-Under. Repeat to fuse green fabric squares together and blue fabric squares together.

3. Trace entire light bulb pattern (including base) onto wrong (white) side of 4 yellow squares. Cut out shapes along pattern lines. Cut 1 (2") square from Wonder-Under. Aligning edges, press Wonder-Under square onto wrong (white) side of remaining yellow square. Do *not* remove paper backing.

4. Trace light bulb pattern (leaving off base) onto wrong side of red, green, and blue squares and remaining yellow square. Cut out shapes along pattern lines. Remove paper backing.

5. Aligning edges, fuse red light bulb to right side of 1 yellow light bulb with base. Repeat to fuse green, blue, and yellow light bulbs to remaining yellow light bulbs with bases. Trim edges if necessary.

6. Referring to photo, use black paint pen to outline lights and to add details. Let dry.

7. Hot-glue 1 light to each button cover.

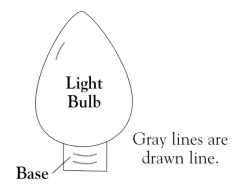

Light Bulb

Base

Gray lines are drawn line.

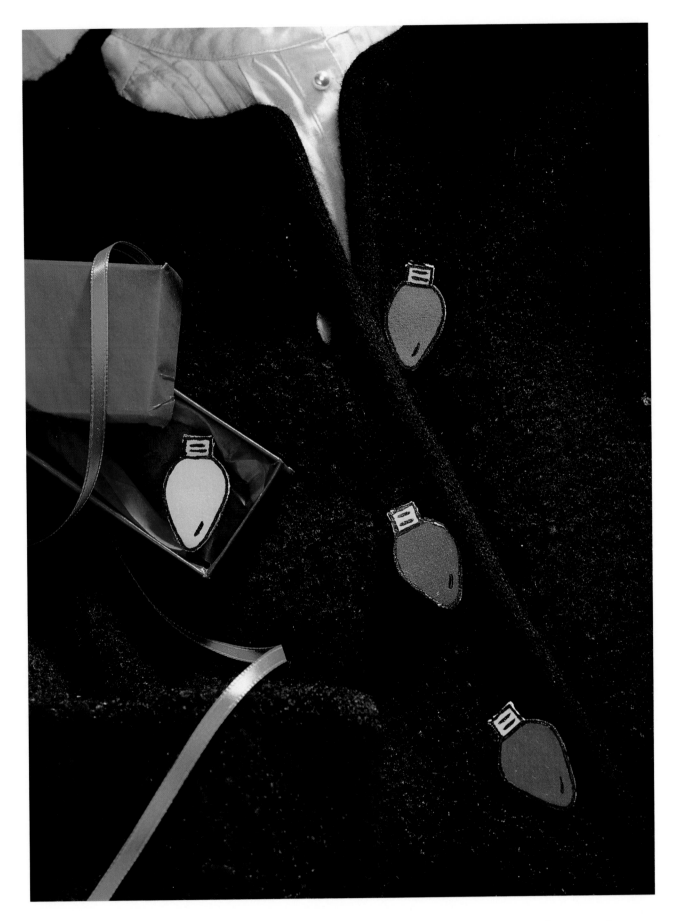

Burlap Bell Pin

*R*ing in the holidays with this cheery pin. Because it's so quick and inexpensive to make, fashion one for yourself and several more for friends.

Materials (for 1 pin)
3" x 9" piece red posterboard
Pellon® Heavy Duty Wonder-Under®
6" square paper
3" square red burlap
Craft glue
Jute twine
Straight pins
Bar pin

Instructions

1. Trace pattern onto posterboard 3 times. Cut out shapes. Cut 3 (3") squares from Wonder-Under.

2. Place paper square onto ironing surface to protect it. Center and press 1 Wonder-Under square onto 1 posterboard bell. Following bell outline, trim Wonder-Under. Remove paper backing. With edges aligned, position second posterboard bell on top of first. Fuse bells together. Center and press second Wonder-Under square on top of second bell. Trim Wonder-Under as before. Remove paper backing. With edges aligned, position remaining posterboard bell on top of second bell. Fuse together. Press final Wonder-Under square on top of last bell. Trim as before. Remove paper backing.

3. Center burlap square on top of final layer of Wonder-Under. Fuse burlap square and layered posterboard bells together. Following bell outline, trim burlap.

4. Apply glue along edges of bell. Referring to photo and beginning and ending at top of bell, press twine into glue and trim. Use straight pins to hold twine in place. Tie length of twine in knot and trim ends close to knot. Fold ends under knot and glue knot in place at base of bell for clapper. Hold in place with straight pins. Tie length of twine in bow and trim ends. Glue bow in place at top of bell. Hold in place with straight pins. Let dry.

5. Remove straight pins and turn bell over. Glue bar pin to back of bell. Let dry.

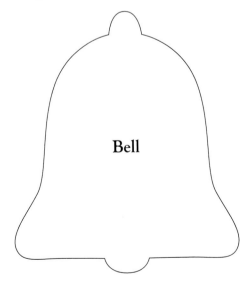

Bell

Wondrous Wearables

Have a Christmas party coming up and don't know what to wear? You're sure to spot the solution in this chapter. There are festive holiday fashions for the whole family—Mom, Dad, and the kids!

Page 142

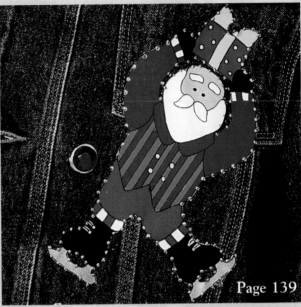

Page 139

Page 118

Page 108

Frosty in the Forest Sweatshirt

$\mathcal{W}$hether wrapping holiday packages or sipping cocoa by a cozy fire, you'll be comfy all winter in this festive sweatshirt.

Materials

Purchased plain sweatshirt
Fabrics: 3½" x 5½" piece white, 7" x
    14½" piece dark green, 4" x 6"
    piece red
13½" length 1⅜"-wide plaid ribbon
7½" length 1¼"-wide dark green
    grosgrain ribbon
1 yard Pellon® Heavy Duty Wonder-
    Under®
Aluminum foil
Cardboard covered with waxed paper
Dimensional fabric paints in squeeze
    bottle: black, orange

Instructions

1. Wash, dry, and iron sweatshirt, fabrics, and ribbons. Do not use fabric softener in washer or dryer.

2. Trace 1 snowman, 5 trees, 5 large hearts, and 1 small heart onto paper side of Wonder-Under. Leaving approximate ½" margin, cut around Wonder-Under shapes. Referring to photo for colors, press shapes onto wrong side of fabric pieces. Cut out shapes along pattern lines. Remove paper backing.

3. Cut 1 (1⅜" x 13½") strip and 1 (1¼" x 7½") strip from Wonder-Under. Cover ironing board with large piece of aluminum foil (shiny side up). Press Wonder-Under strips onto wrong side of corresponding ribbon lengths.

4. For base piece, cut 9¾" length from 1⅜"-wide ribbon. Trace 1 hat onto Wonder-Under side of remaining length of 1⅜"-wide ribbon. Cut out hat shape along pattern lines. Trace 5 trunks onto Wonder-Under side of 1¼"-wide ribbon. Cut out shapes along pattern lines. Remove paper backing.

5. Referring to photo, position appliqués on sweatshirt front. Fuse shapes in place.

6. Place cardboard covered with waxed paper inside sweatshirt. Referring to photo and using black dimensional fabric paint, draw snowman's eyes, mouth, buttons, and arms. Using orange dimensional fabric paint, draw carrot nose. Let dry. Let paint dry for 24 hours.

7. Refer to paint manufacturer's instructions to launder sweatshirt.

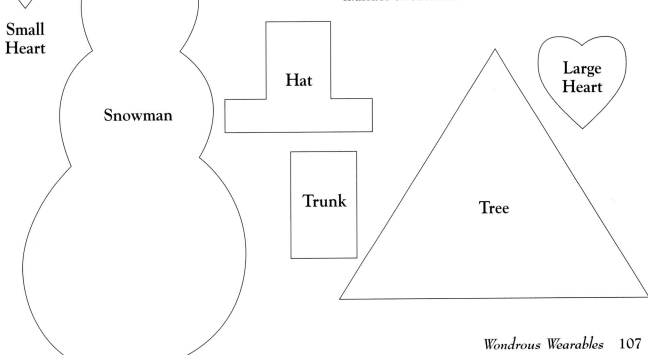

Small Heart

Snowman

Hat

Trunk

Tree

Large Heart

Gingerbread Garland Sweatshirt

$\mathcal{E}$veryone, including Santa, loves gingerbread men! Although this quick-to-make appliquéd shirt features dimensional fabric paint designs, no special painting skills are required.

Materials

Purchased sweatshirt
Fabric scraps for appliqué
1⅓ yards ¹⁄₁₆"-wide satin ribbon
¼ yard lightweight fusible interfacing
¾ yard Pellon® Heavy Duty Wonder-Under®
Cardboard covered with waxed paper
Dimensional fabric paints in squeeze bottles: black, red, iridescent glitter, brown
Disappearing-ink fabric marker
Liquid ravel preventer
Washable fabric glue

Instructions

1. Wash, dry, and iron sweatshirt, fabrics, and ribbon. Do not use fabric softener in washer or dryer.

2. Press fusible interfacing onto wrong side of white fabric scraps. Trace 2 coat cuffs and 1 each of remaining pattern shapes on pages 110 and 111, except gingerbread man, onto paper side of Wonder-Under. Leaving approximate ½" margin, cut around Wonder-Under shapes. Referring to photo for colors, press shapes onto wrong side of fabric scraps. Cut out shapes along pattern lines.

3. Referring to photo, position appliqués on sweatshirt front in order indicated on pattern pieces. Fuse shapes in place.

4. Place cardboard covered with waxed paper inside sweatshirt. Referring to photo and using black dimensional fabric paint, outline boots, gloves, and belt and then paint eyes. Let dry. Using red dimensional fabric paint, outline hat, coat, and pants and then paint nose. Let dry. Using iridescent glitter dimensional fabric paint, outline beard, face, mouth, mustache, hair, hat trim, star, coat cuffs, coat trim, and pants cuffs and then paint eyebrows. Let dry. Cut out a paper gingerbread man pattern. Using disappearing-ink fabric marker and referring to photo, trace gingerbread man to make garland of 12 gingerbread men between Santa's hands. Use brown dimensional fabric paint to paint garland. Let all paints dry for 24 hours.

5. Cut 12 (4") lengths of ribbon. Tie each length in bow. Trim ends as desired. Apply small amount of liquid ravel preventer to cut ends of ribbon. Let dry. Referring to photo, glue a bow to each gingerbread man neck.

6. To launder sweatshirt, refer to paint manufacturer's instructions.

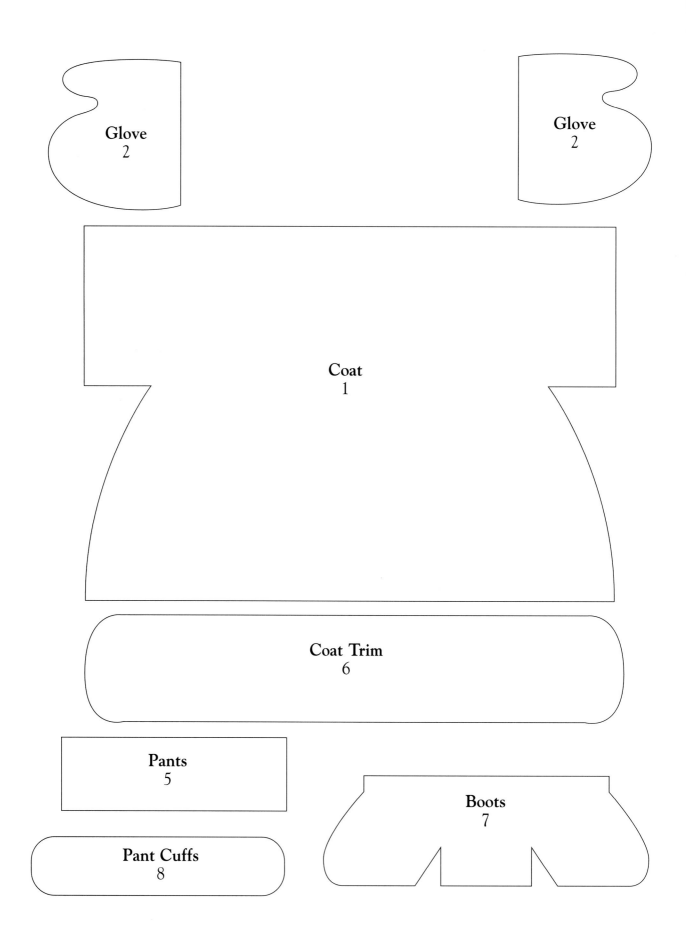

Glove
2

Glove
2

Coat
1

Coat Trim
6

Pants
5

Pant Cuffs
8

Boots
7

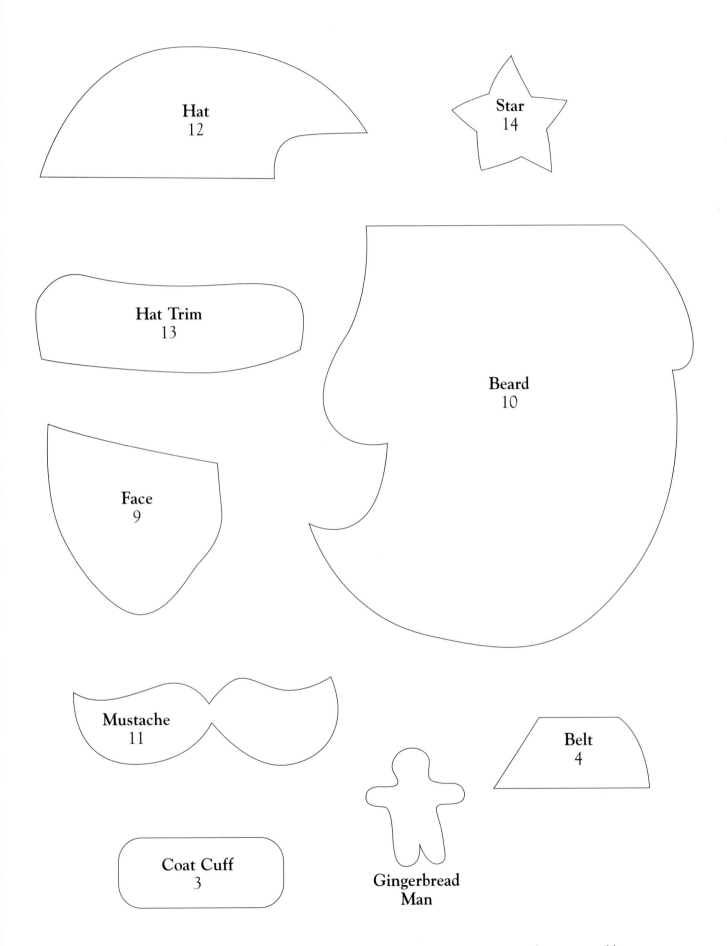

Toy Soldier Tie

Add a touch of holiday fun to Dad's wardrobe. He'll love this tie for casual Fridays at the office during the holiday season.

Materials

- Pellon® Wonder-Under®
- 5" x 12" piece peach fabric
- Fabric scraps: black, blue, striped, green
- Purchased necktie large enough to accommodate 3¼" x 10⅞" design

Instructions

1. For soldier base, press Wonder-Under onto wrong side of peach fabric. Do *not* remove paper backing. Trace soldier outline on page 114 onto right side of peach fabric. Cut out.

2. Using patterns on pages 112–114, trace 1 hat, 1 hat trim, 1 plume, 2 hair (1 in reverse), 1 mustache, 1 beard, 2 eyebrows (1 in reverse), 2 eyes, 1 belt, 1 coat, 2 epaulets (1 in reverse), 1 pants, and 1 boots onto paper side of Wonder-Under. Leaving approximate ½" margin, cut around shapes.

3. Press hat trim, hair, eyes, eyebrows, mustache, beard, belt, and boots onto wrong side of black fabric and pants onto wrong side of blue fabric. Press coat onto wrong side of striped fabric, positioning shape so that stripes run vertically. Press epaulets and hat onto wrong side of striped fabric, positioning shapes so that stripes run horizontally. Press plume onto wrong side of green fabric. Cut out shapes along pattern lines. Remove paper backing.

4. Arrange shapes on right side of peach outline in order indicated on pattern pieces. Fuse shapes in place.

5. Remove paper backing from soldier base. Referring to photo, fuse soldier to tie.

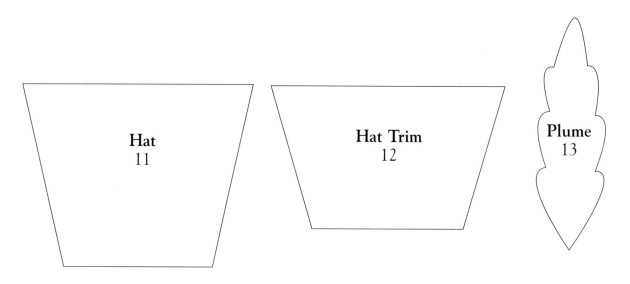

Hat
11

Hat Trim
12

Plume
13

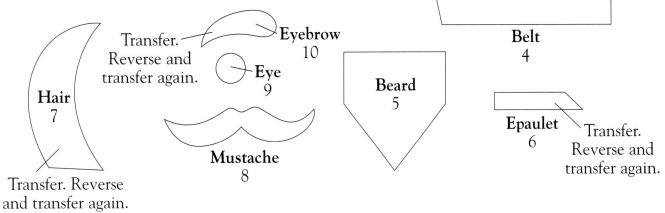

Hair
7

Transfer. Reverse
and transfer again.

Transfer.
Reverse and
transfer again.

Eyebrow
10

Eye
9

Mustache
8

Beard
5

Belt
4

Epaulet
6

Transfer.
Reverse and
transfer again.

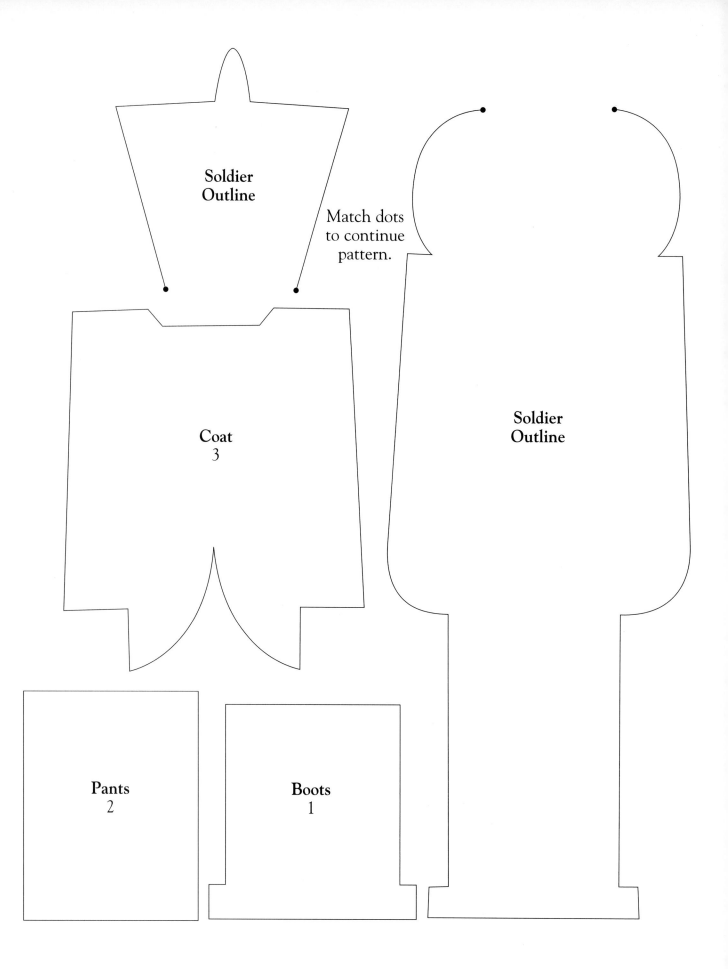

Soldier
Outline

Match dots
to continue
pattern.

Coat
3

Soldier
Outline

Pants
2

Boots
1

Crescent Santa Sweatshirt

This shirt is for any Kris Kringle fan who thinks Santa hung the moon and the stars! A touch of gold lamé gives it a bit of sparkle.

Materials

Purchased sweatshirt
Fabrics: 11" square white solid for beard and mustache, 7½" x 4½" piece red for hat, 5½" x 2½" white print for hat trim, 3½" square cream for face, 3½" square gold lamé for star
1 yard Pellon® Heavy Duty Wonder-Under®
Cardboard covered in waxed paper
Dimensional fabric paints in squeeze bottles: iridescent glitter, gold glitter, red, peach
Small paintbrush
Peach fabric paint
Paper towel
Permanent rhinestone adhesive
2 (7-mm) acrylic rhinestones for eyes

Instructions

1. Wash, dry, and iron sweatshirt and fabrics. Do not use fabric softener in washer or dryer.

2. Trace each pattern piece onto paper side of Wonder-Under. Leaving approximate ½" margin, cut around Wonder-Under shapes.

Referring to photo for colors, press shapes onto wrong side of fabric pieces. Cut out shapes along pattern lines.

3. Lay sweatshirt faceup on ironing board. Referring to photo, arrange appliqué shapes on sweatshirt in order indicated on pattern pieces. Fuse shapes in place.

4. Place cardboard covered with waxed paper inside sweatshirt. Outline mustache and beard with iridescent glitter paint. Let dry. Outline hat trim and star with gold glitter paint. Let dry. Outline hat with red paint. Let dry. Use peach dimensional paint to draw nose. Let dry. For cheeks and mouth, dip paintbrush into peach fabric paint. Stroke brush on paper towel until almost all paint is removed. Referring to photo, brush paint on fabric to make cheeks and mouth. Let dry.

5. Referring to photo and using rhinestone adhesive, glue rhinestones to Santa's face for eyes. Let dry.

6. To launder sweatshirt, refer to paint and glue manufacturer's instructions.

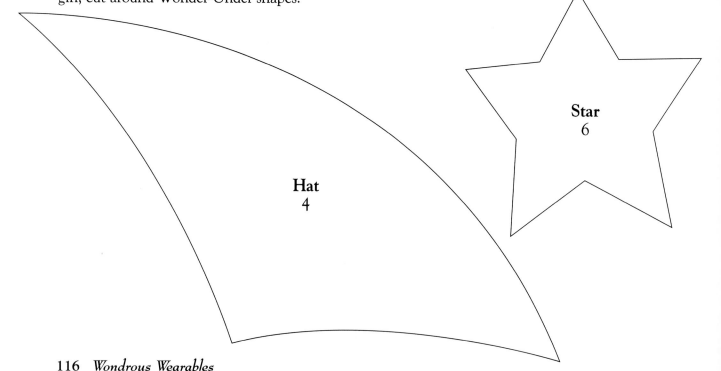

Hat
4

Star
6

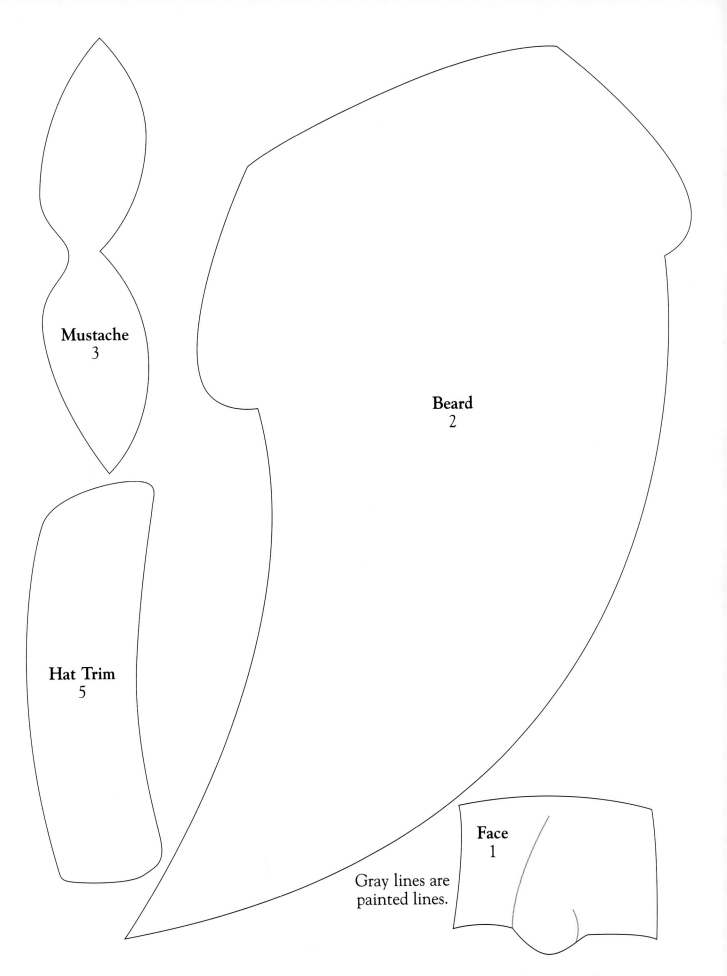

Mustache
3

Beard
2

Hat Trim
5

Face
1

Gray lines are
painted lines.

Snowman Vest

$\mathcal{D}$ecorate the front of a purchased denim vest with this fun-loving snowman. You may want to replace the buttons on your vest with brightly colored ones that coordinate with your appliqué fabrics.

Materials

Purchased denim vest
Fabrics: 6" x 7" piece white for snowman, 2½" x 4" piece red print for
  hat, 2½" square red for mitten,
  1" square orange for nose, 3" square
  black print for boot, 2½" x 3½"
  piece each of 3 different greens for
  tree, 1¼" x 7" strip yellow-and-black
  plaid for scarf
Pellon® Heavy Duty Wonder-Under®
Medium-tip permanent black fabric
  marker
Fabric glue
1 (1"-diameter) white pom-pom
Small safety pin

Instructions

1. Wash, dry, and iron vest and fabrics. Do not use fabric softener in washer or dryer.

2. Trace patterns below and on page 120 onto paper side of Wonder-Under. Leaving approximate ½" margin, cut around shapes. Referring to photo for colors, press shapes onto wrong side of appliqué fabrics. Cut out shapes along pattern lines. Remove paper backing.

3. Referring to photo, arrange shapes on left side of vest front in order indicated on pattern pieces. Fuse shapes in place.

4. Refer to photo and use black marker to outline shapes and to draw eye, mouth, and line for trunk from tree to snowman's hand.

5. Glue pom-pom to point of hat. Let dry.

6. For scarf, knot center of yellow-and-black plaid strip; fray ends. Working from underside of vest, pin scarf to snowman's neck.

7. Before laundering, remove scarf. Then refer to glue manufacturer's instructions.

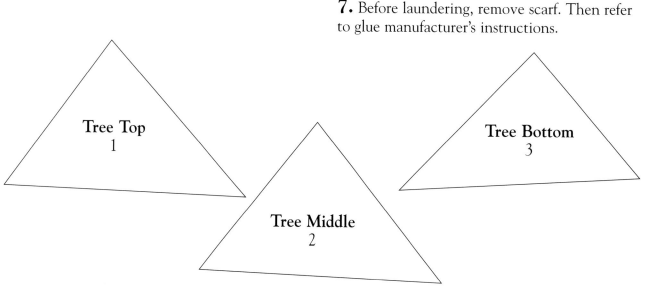

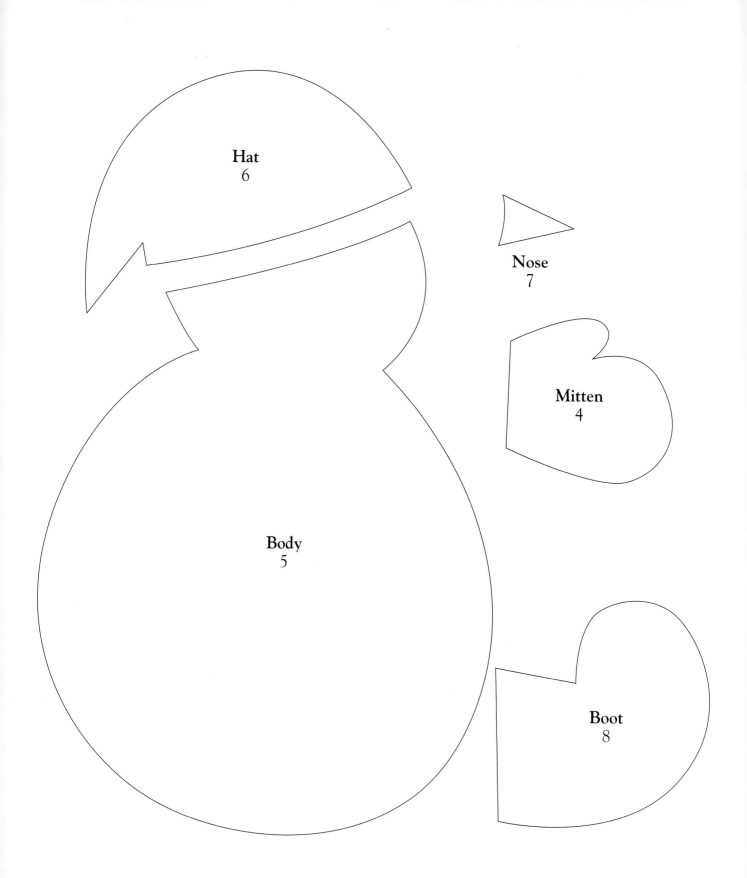

Hat
6

Nose
7

Mitten
4

Body
5

Boot
8

Wintry Forest Sweatshirt

Here's the ideal shirt to wear while searching for the
perfect Christmas tree.

Materials

Purchased sweatshirt
Fabrics: 13½" x 12" piece blue with
  white dots, 13" x 9" piece green with
  white dots, 4" square gold lamé
Green grosgrain ribbons: 1 (3") length
  2¼"-wide, 2 (13") lengths 1½"-wide
1¼ yards Pellon® Heavy Duty Wonder-
  Under®
Aluminum foil
Liquid ravel preventer
Cardboard covered with waxed paper
Dimensional fabric paints in squeeze
  bottles: blue, green, gold

Instructions

1. Wash, dry, and iron sweatshirt, fabrics, and ribbons. Do not use fabric softener in washer or dryer.

2. Trace 3 skies, 3 stars, and 3 trees onto paper side of Wonder-Under. Leaving approximate ½" margin, cut around Wonder-Under shapes. Press skies onto wrong side of blue fabric, trees onto wrong side of green fabric, and stars onto wrong side of gold lamé. Cut out shapes along pattern lines. Remove paper backing.

3. Cut 1 (2¼" x 3") strip and 2 (1½" x 13") strips from Wonder-Under. Cover ironing board with large piece of aluminum foil (shiny side up). Press Wonder-Under strips onto 1 side of corresponding ribbon lengths. Coat cut ends of ribbon with liquid ravel preventer.

4. For trunks, trace pattern 3 times onto Wonder-Under side of 2¼"-wide ribbon. Cut out shapes along pattern lines. Remove paper backing from all ribbon pieces.

5. Lay sweatshirt faceup on ironing board. Referring to photo, position ribbon pieces and fabric appliqués on front of sweatshirt. Fuse shapes in place.

6. Place cardboard covered with waxed paper inside sweatshirt. Use blue fabric paint to outline skies. Let dry. Use green fabric paint to outline trees, trunks, and base ribbon pieces. Let dry. Use gold fabric paint to outline stars. Let dry.

7. To launder sweatshirt, refer to paint manufacturer's instructions.

Other Ideas

This tree motif works very well for a bellpull. From blue felt, cut a background piece measuring approximately 4" x 11". Fold 1" of the top edge of the felt piece back to make a casing and fuse it in place. Cut the tree motif from green fabric and fuse it to the center of the felt. Use white fabric paint to add snowflakes. Insert a bellpull rod through the casing and then add a cording hanger.

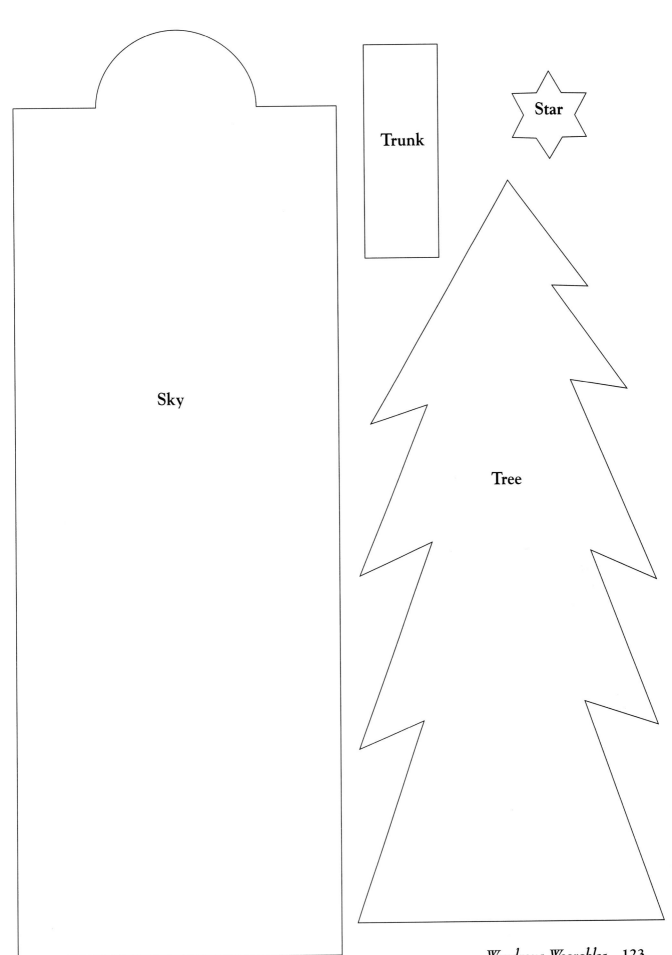

Sky

Trunk

Star

Tree

Pretty Package Collars

Your little angels will look picture-perfect in these easy-to-make Christmas collars.

Materials (for 1 collar)

Aluminum foil
¾"-wide Pellon® Wonder-Under® fusible tape
Matching ribbon lengths: ¾ yard each ¾"- and 1½"-wide
Purchased plain white square-edged collar
Liquid ravel preventer
Safety pin

Instructions

1. Cover ironing board with a large piece of aluminum foil (shiny side up). Cut 1 (27") length from fusible tape. Press fusible tape length onto wrong side of ¾"-wide ribbon length. Remove paper backing.

2. Referring to photo, center ¾"-wide ribbon length vertically on collar front and trim to fit; do *not* fuse in place yet. Center remaining ¾"-wide ribbon length horizontally on collar front and trim to fit; do *not* fuse in place yet. Coat cut ends of ribbon lengths with liquid ravel preventer. Let dry. Fuse ribbon lengths in place.

3. Tie 1½"-wide ribbon length in bow and notch ends. Coat notched ends with liquid ravel preventer. Let dry. Working from underside of collar, pin bow to collar front at intersection of ¾"-wide ribbon lengths.

Other Ideas

For an elegant Christmas table setting, fuse ribbon lengths to plain white linen place mats, using the same technique you used to make these collars. Offset the ribbons so that the intersection of the lengths is in the lower right-hand corner of the place mat. Pin a ribbon bow to the center of the intersection.

Smiling Snowman Sweatshirt

You don't have to wait for the first snowfall to make this snowman. Fused fabric shapes, dimensional paints, and buttons make for an easy project. White sweatpants complete the snowman look.

Materials

Purchased white sweatshirt
Fabrics: 4" x 8½" piece black, 2" x 4" piece orange
Grosgrain ribbons: 4" length ⅞"-wide red with small black polka-dots, 9" length 1½"-wide red with large black polka-dots, 2" length ⅜"-wide red with small black polka-dots
Liquid ravel preventer
Pellon® Heavy Duty Wonder-Under®
Aluminum foil
Cardboard covered with waxed paper
Dimensional fabric paints in squeeze bottles: black, orange
Clear acetate
Permanent black marker
Hole punch
Small paintbrush
Black fabric paint
Fabric glue
2 (1⅛") square black buttons
Small safety pin

Instructions

1. Wash, dry, and iron sweatshirt, fabrics, and ribbons. Do not use fabric softener in washer or dryer. Coat cut ends of ribbons with liquid ravel preventer. Let dry.

2. Trace hat pattern and nose pattern on page 129 onto paper side of Wonder-Under. Leaving approximate ½" margin, cut around shapes. Press hat shape onto wrong side of black fabric and nose shape onto wrong side of orange fabric. Cut out shapes along pattern lines. Do *not* remove paper backing.

3. Cut 1 (⅞" x 4") strip from Wonder-Under. Cover ironing board with a large piece of aluminum foil (shiny side up). Press Wonder-Under strip onto wrong side of ⅞"-wide ribbon length. Remove paper backing.

4. For hatband, referring to photo and pattern for placement, fuse ⅞"-wide ribbon length onto right side of hat. Remove paper backing from hat and nose. Referring to photo and pattern for placement, position hat and nose on front of sweatshirt. Fuse in place.

5. Place cardboard covered with waxed paper inside sweatshirt. Outline hat with black dimensional fabric paint and outline nose with orange dimensional fabric paint. Let dry.

6. To make mouth stencil, place acetate over pattern. Mark mouth dots on acetate, using black marker. Use hole punch to punch out marked mouth dots. Referring to photo and pattern for placement, position acetate mouth stencil on front of sweatshirt. Use small paintbrush and black fabric paint to paint mouth. Let dry.

7. Referring to photo and pattern for placement, glue button eyes in place on front of sweatshirt. Let dry.

8. For bow tie, glue ends of 1½"-wide ribbon length together, forming circle. Pinch center of ribbon circle together, forming 2 loops. Wrap ⅜"-wide ribbon length around center and glue to secure. Trim ends if necessary. Center seam at back of bow. Center bow 2" below snowman's mouth. Working from inside of sweatshirt, pin ribbon bow tie in place.

9. To launder, remove bow tie and refer to paint and glue manufacturer's instructions.

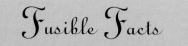

Fusible Facts

When fusing onto wearables, there are several tips you should keep in mind.

- **Always prewash.** Wash all of your fabrics as well as the garment onto which you will be fusing. Washing will remove the sizing that prevents fusible web from bonding with the fabric.

- **Do not use fabric softener** in the washer or the dryer. Fabric softeners also prevent the fusible web from bonding with the fabric.

- **Finish the edges** of your appliqué to ensure a washable garment. One such edge finish is washable fabric paint. (See Embellishment Techniques, page 8.)

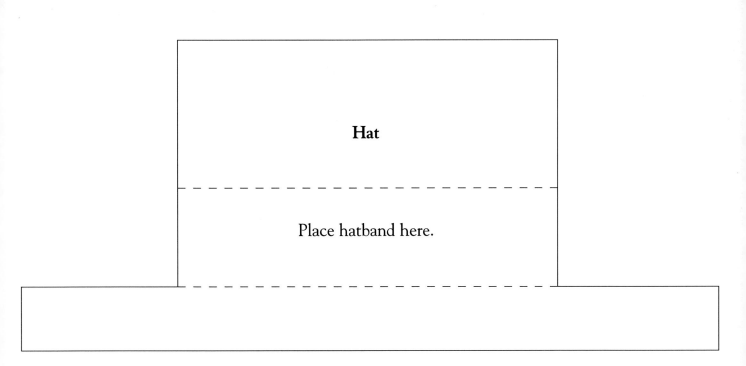

Hat

Place hatband here.

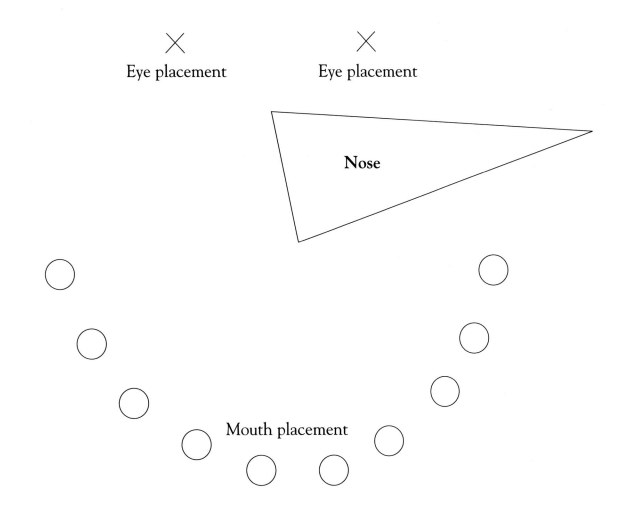

Eye placement   Eye placement

Nose

Mouth placement

Christmas in the Kitchen

You'll be cooking up lots of holiday spirit when you don this cheery wreath apron.

Materials

Purchased solid-colored apron with bib
Scraps of green fabrics for appliqués
Torn 2¾" x 24" strip red plaid fabric
    for bow
Pellon® Heavy Duty Wonder-Under®
    scraps
6"-diameter plate
Disappearing-ink fabric marker
Green dimensional fabric paint in
    squeeze bottle
Safety pin

Instructions

1. Wash and dry apron and fabrics; do not use fabric softener in washer or dryer.

2. Trace leaf pattern 27 times onto paper side of Wonder-Under, spacing shapes at least ½" apart. Leaving approximate ¼" margin, cut around shapes. Press leaf shapes onto wrong side of green fabric scraps. Cut out shapes along pattern lines. Remove paper backing.

3. Measure 2½" from top of apron and center plate facedown. Trace plate with disappearing-ink fabric marker. Arrange leaf appliqués as desired, using circle as guide. Fuse leaves in place.

4. Outline leaves, using dimensional fabric paint. Let dry 24 hours.

5. Tie red plaid fabric strip in bow. Using safety pin and working from back of apron, pin bow to top front of wreath.

6. To launder, remove bow. Then follow paint manufacturer's instructions.

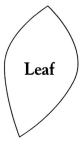

Leaf

Fusible Fact

For most wearables it is best to use regular-weight web, as heavyweight web may add too much stiffness. However, for some projects—such as this one where the garment you are embellishing is made from a heavy, stiff fabric—heavyweight web is a better choice since it will ensure a stronger bond.

Roly-Poly
Santa Sweatshirt

This sweatshirt has a playful touch of whimsy that will delight a little boy or girl.

Materials
Purchased sweatshirt
Fabrics: white; red print for coat, arms, and hat; green print; black-and-white check; black; red solid; pink
Ribbons: 4" length ⅜"-wide red grosgrain with white polka-dots, 9" length ⅛"-wide black satin, 6" length ⅝"-wide black grosgrain
Dimensional fabric paints in squeeze bottle: gold glitter, iridescent glitter, red glitter, pink, black
Small paintbrush
Ultrafine gold glitter
1 yard Pellon® Heavy Duty Wonder-Under®
Liquid ravel preventer
Washable fabric glue
Cardboard covered with waxed paper
Permanent rhinestone adhesive
Acrylic rhinestones: 2 (5-mm) green for eyes, 2 (7-mm) clear for wheels

Instructions

1. Wash, dry, and iron sweatshirt, fabrics, and ribbons. Do not use fabric softener in washer or dryer.

2. Cut 3" square from white fabric. Using gold glitter paint and paintbrush, paint 1 side of white square. While paint is still wet, generously sprinkle gold glitter on paint. Let dry.

Shake off excess glitter. Trace star pattern on page 134 onto wrong side of painted fabric square. Cut out and set aside.

3. Trace 1 each of following pattern pieces on pages 134 and 135 onto paper side of Wonder-Under: pom-pom, hat, hat trim, face, beard, coat, arm pulling horse, arm holding wand, saddle, mane, forelock, horse, and tail. Trace 2 each of following pattern pieces onto paper side of Wonder-Under: cuff, glove, and wheel. Leaving approximate ½" margin, cut around Wonder-Under shapes. Referring to photo for colors, press shapes onto interfacing side of fabric pieces. Cut out shapes along pattern lines.

4. Lay sweatshirt faceup on ironing board. Referring to photo, arrange appliqué shapes on sweatshirt in order indicated on pattern pieces. Do *not* fuse in place.

5. Coat cut ends of ribbons with liquid ravel preventer. Position ⅜"-wide polka-dot ribbon under wheels for base of horse. Cut ⅛"-wide satin ribbon length in half. Position 1 satin ribbon length under hand for wand. Position remaining satin ribbon length under cuff on coat and under base of horse. Position ⅝"-wide black ribbon length under arm for belt. Position gold glitter star at top of wand. Using fabric glue, glue star and all ribbons to sweatshirt. Let dry.

6. Fuse appliqués to sweatshirt. Place cardboard covered with waxed paper inside sweatshirt. Outline star with gold glitter paint. Let dry. Referring to photo, outline pom-pom, hat trim, beard, and cuffs with iridescent glitter paint. For heart on saddle, squeeze 2 dots of iridescent glitter paint side by side. Use tip of bottle to pull some paint from each dot to form point. Let dry. Outline hat, coat, arms, and saddle with red glitter paint. Let dry. Outline

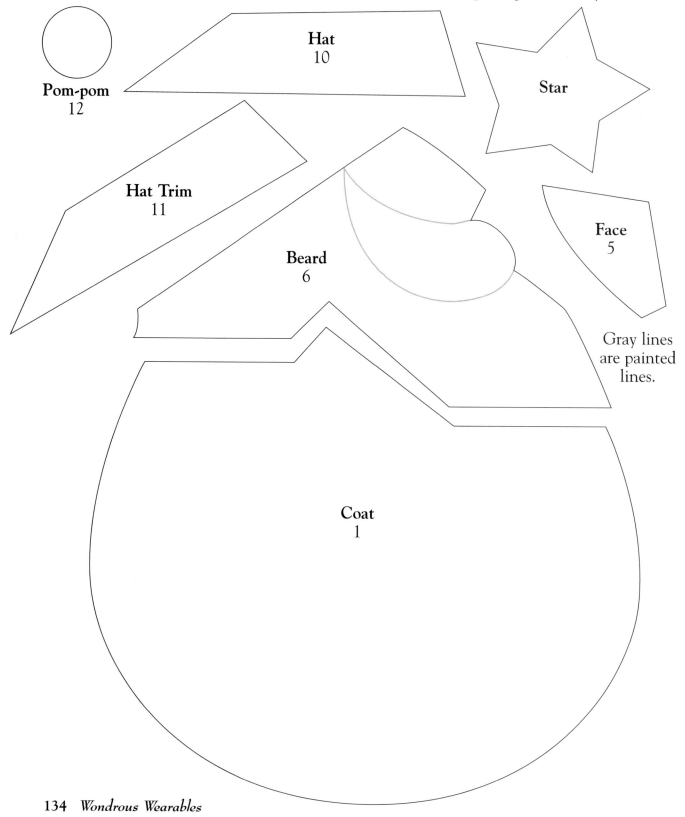

Pom-pom
12

Hat
10

Star

Hat Trim
11

Beard
6

Face
5

Gray lines
are painted
lines.

Coat
1

face with pink paint. Let dry. Outline gloves, horse, mane, forelock, tail, and wheels with black paint. Let dry.

7. Referring to photo and using rhinestone adhesive, glue 5-mm green stones to Santa's face and horse's face for eyes; glue 7-mm clear stones to wheels. Let dry.

8. To launder sweatshirt, refer to paint and glue manufacturer's instructions.

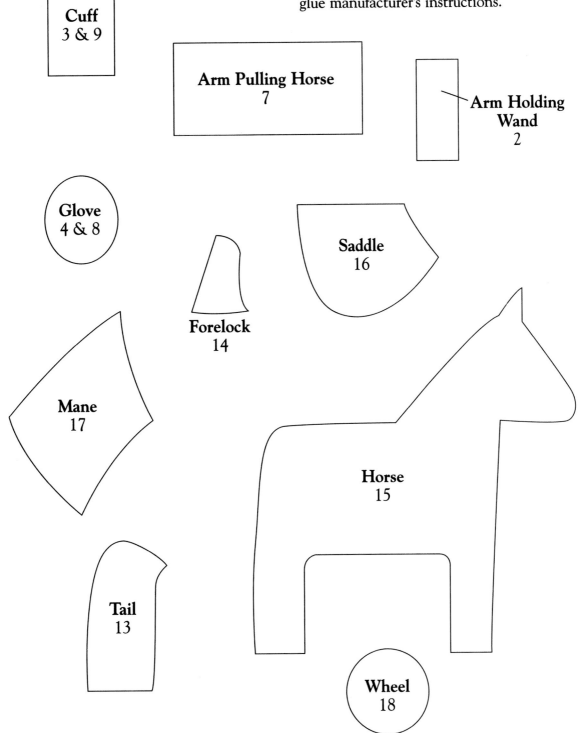

Cuff
3 & 9

Arm Pulling Horse
7

**Arm Holding
Wand**
2

Glove
4 & 8

Saddle
16

Forelock
14

Mane
17

Horse
15

Tail
13

Wheel
18

Snowman Romper

*K*eep your tyke warm and toasty in this romper,
featuring Frosty himself.

Materials

Pellon® Wonder-Under®
Fabric scraps: white, black
Purchased romper
Dimensional fabric paints in squeeze
    bottles: white, black, orange
10" length 1"-wide plaid ribbon
Thread to match ribbon
Washable fabric glue
White pom-poms: ½"-diameter,
    ⅜"-diameter

Instructions

1. Wash, dry, and iron sweatshirt, fabrics, and ribbons. Do not use fabric softener in washer or dryer.

2. Trace patterns on page 138 onto paper side of Wonder-Under. Leaving approximate ½" margin, cut around shapes. Press snowman body shapes onto wrong side of white fabric; press hat shape onto wrong side of black fabric. Cut out shapes along pattern lines. Remove paper backing.

3. Referring to photo, position appliqués on leg of romper. Fuse appliqués in place.

4. Using white fabric paint, outline edges of snowman body appliqués. Using black fabric paint, outline edges of snowman hat and draw eyes, mouth, arms, and buttons. Using orange fabric paint, draw carrot nose. Let dry.

5. For scarf, fringe ends of ribbon ¼". Wrap thread tightly around center of ribbon. Knot thread and trim ends close to knot. Matching ends, fold ribbon in half. Wrap thread tightly around ribbon 1¾" from center knot. Knot thread and trim ends close to knot. Position scarf on snowman and glue in place. Let dry.

6. For snow, glue pom-poms as desired onto romper. Let dry.

7. To launder, follow paint and glue manufacturer's instructions.

Other Ideas

Any plain winterwear would be a good background for this frosty motif. For example, fuse the full length of the snowman to the ends of a scarf and then fuse just his head and hat to earmuffs. Embellish the appliqués just as you did for the romper.

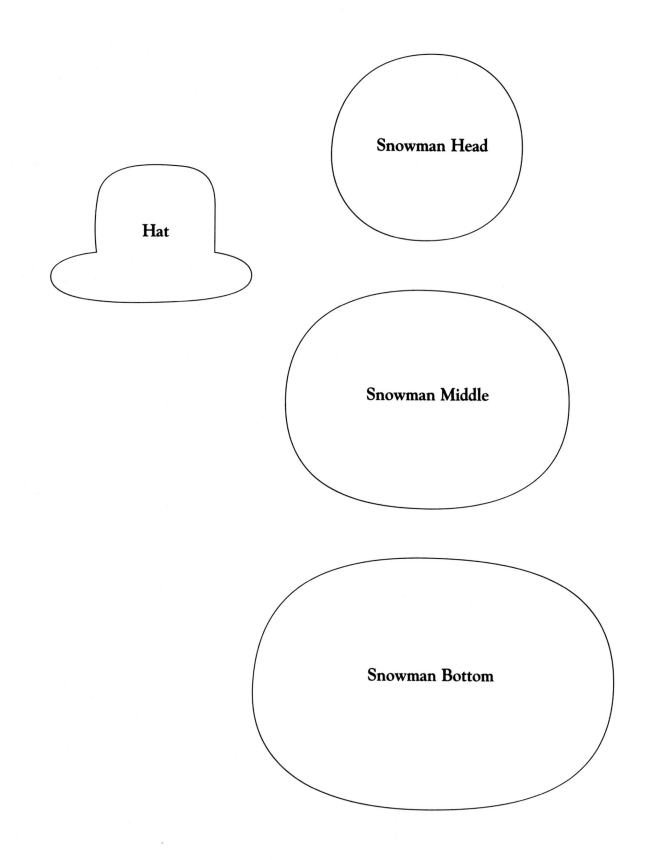

Seasonal Motifs Jacket

This jazzed-up jean jacket will show off your Christmas spirit as you run those holiday errands.

Materials

Purchased denim jacket
Fabrics: 4" x 5" striped piece for rectangle behind snowman, variety of scraps for remaining appliqués
Pellon® Heavy Duty Wonder-Under®
Medium-tip permanent black fabric marker
Dimensional fabric paints in squeeze bottles: gold, white
Permanent rhinestone adhesive
Acrylic rhinestone gems: 5 large red, 7 small golden
Fabric glue
Gold soutache braid

Instructions

1. Wash, dry, and iron jacket and fabrics. Do not use fabric softener in washer or dryer.

2. Trace individual pieces of each desired motif onto paper side of Wonder-Under. Leaving approximate ½" margin, cut around shapes. Also cut 4" x 5" piece of Wonder-Under. Referring to photo for colors, press shapes onto wrong side of fabric scraps. Cut out shapes along pattern lines. Press 4" x 5" piece of Wonder-Under onto wrong side of 4" x 5" striped fabric rectangle. Remove paper backing.

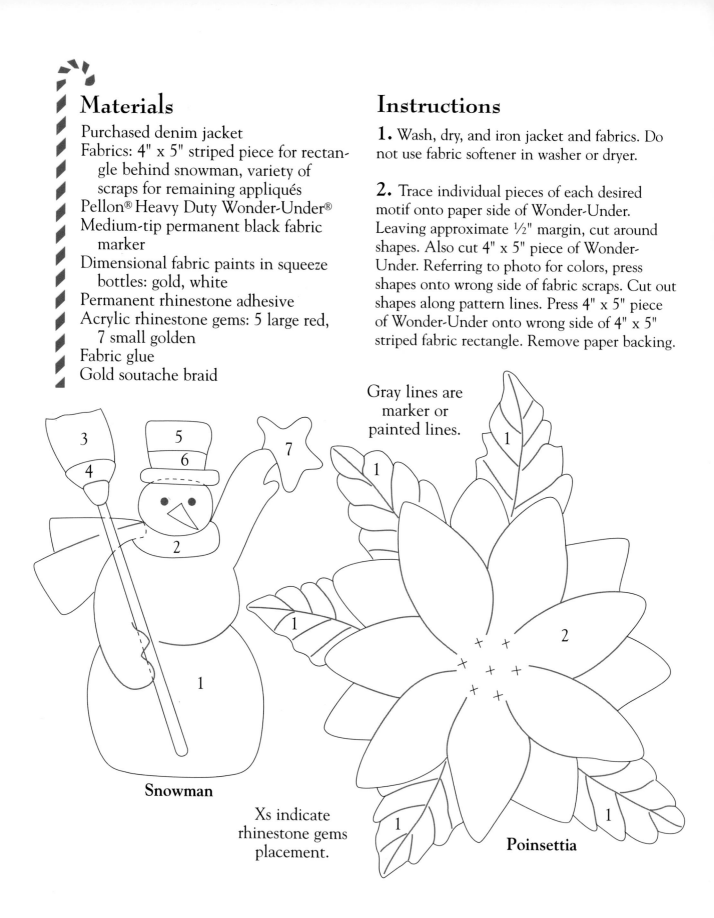

Gray lines are marker or painted lines.

Snowman

Xs indicate rhinestone gems placement.

Poinsettia

3. Referring to photo and patterns, fuse motifs where desired on jacket front in order indicated on each individual motif. (For snowman, fuse striped fabric rectangle first and then fuse snowman on top.)

4. Referring to photo, use black marker, gold fabric paint, and white fabric paint to embellish motifs and to add details. Let dry. Use gold paint to embellish jacket if desired. Let dry.

5. Use rhinestone adhesive to glue large red acrylic gems to jacket front as desired; glue small golden rhinestones to center of poinsettia. Use fabric glue to glue soutache braid to jacket collar, pocket flaps, and waistband.

6. To launder, refer to glue and paint manufacturer's instructions.

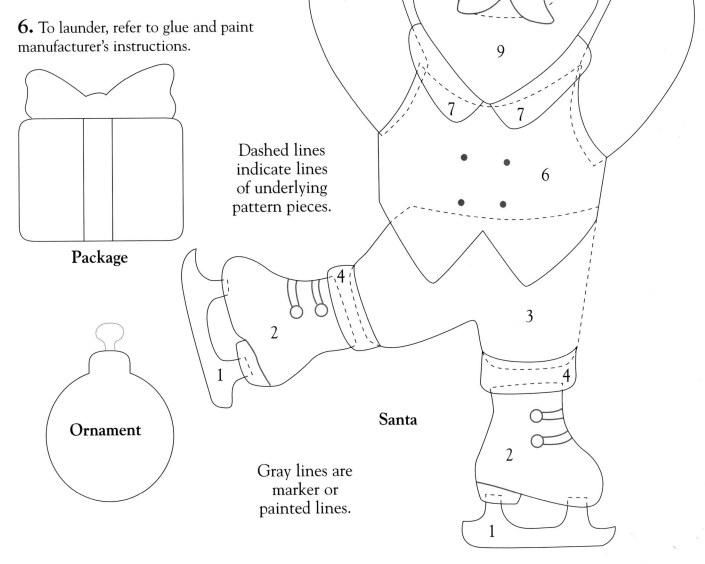

Package

Ornament

Dashed lines indicate lines of underlying pattern pieces.

Santa

Gray lines are marker or painted lines.

Ribbon Bedecked Nightshirt

This embellished tee makes great sleepwear for a young girl. Add a pair of purchased plaid flannel boxer shorts for a set of pj's that are ideal for holiday slumber parties!

Materials

Purchased T-shirt
Ribbons: 1 yard length ⅜"-wide black grosgrain with white polka-dots, ⅞ yard length 1½"-wide plaid, ½ yard length ⅞"-wide red grosgrain with black polka-dots
Pellon® Wonder-Under®
Aluminum foil
Liquid ravel preventer
Small safety pin
Washable fabric glue
4 (¾") red buttons

Instructions

1. Wash, dry, and iron T-shirt and ribbons. Do not use fabric softener in washer or dryer.

2. Cut 25" length from ⅜"-wide ribbon. From Wonder-Under, cut 1 (1½" x 31½") strip and 1 (⅜" x 25") strip. Cover ironing board with a large piece of aluminum foil (shiny side up). Press 1½" x 31½" Wonder-Under strip onto wrong side of corresponding plaid ribbon length. Press ⅜" x 25" Wonder-Under strip onto wrong side of 25" length of ⅜"-wide ribbon. Remove paper backing.

3. Cut each fused ribbon length in half. Referring to photo, position ribbon lengths on front of T-shirt in V shape. Trim ends of ribbons an angle to make point of V and to fit shoulder seams. Coat cut ends of ribbons with liquid ravel preventer. Let dry. Fuse ribbons in place.

4. Tie ⅞"-wide ribbon in bow. Trim ends. Tie remaining ⅜"-wide ribbon around center of bow and tie in knot at back of bow. Trim ends of ⅜"-wide ribbon. Working from inside of T-shirt, pin bow to front of T-shirt at point of V made by plaid ribbon.

5. Referring to photo, glue buttons in row down center front of shirt, spacing buttons evenly.

6. To launder, remove bow and refer to glue manufacturer's instructions.

Acknowledgments

SPECIAL THANKS...

...to the following people and companies for their valuable contributions toward project development:

Kendall Boggs

Alice London Cox

Kim Eidson Crane

Frivols

Heidi Tyline King

Duffy Morrison

Betsy Cooper Scott

Carol Tipton

Cynthia Moody Wheeler

Nancy Worrell

We especially want to thank the talented staffs at **Leisure Arts Inc.,** and **Freudenberg Nonwovens,** and in particular **Anne Van Wagner Childs, Gloria Bearden,** and **Jane Schenck.**

ORDERING INFORMATION

To locate a Pellon® Wonder-Under® retailer in your area, call 1-800-223-5275.